Robert W. Warden retired from the Royal Air Force in 1992 after 22 years service as an aircraft technician. After his military career he worked for a further 24 years in the NHS as a nurse before retiring in 2018.

Retirement has enabled Robert to explore writing, painting and music. This is his first published work.

I would like to dedicate this book to all seniors who have reacquainted themselves with their inner child.

Robert W. Warden

MY FRIEND'S PLACE

A senior moment in India

AUSTIN MACAULEY PUBLISHERS™
LONDON • CAMBRIDGE • NEW YORK • SHARJAH

Copyright © Robert W. Warden 2023

The right of Robert W. Warden to be identified as author of this work has been asserted by the author in accordance with sections 77 and 78 of the Copyright, Designs and Patents Act 1988.

All rights reserved. No part of this publication may be reproduced, stored in a retrieval system, or transmitted in any form or by any means, electronic, mechanical, photocopying, recording, or otherwise, without the prior permission of the publishers.

Any person who commits any unauthorised act in relation to this publication may be liable to criminal prosecution and civil claims for damages.

All of the events in this memoir are true to the best of the author's memory. The views expressed in this memoir are solely those of the author.

A CIP catalogue record for this title is available from the British Library.

ISBN 9781035809172 (Paperback)
ISBN 9781035809189 (ePub e-book)

www.austinmacauley.com

First Published 2023
Austin Macauley Publishers Ltd®
1 Canada Square
Canary Wharf
London
E14 5AA

To Carol, for her forbearance and encouragement. Daniel my ever-supportive son. Al and Chris for their helpful comments.

Table of Contents

Introduction	11
1: The Plan	13
2: Cometh the Hour	27
3: To Sleep Perchance to Dream	41
4: India	51
5: The Shoe Shine Boy and the Tailor	65
6: The Mandovi Express	80
7: Goa and the French Connection	98
8: Mini and Nosferatu	111
9: Monkeys, Dogs and Arabian Nights	122
10: The Tour	129
11: Ebony and Ivory	140
12: Gandhi and the One-Eyed Entrepreneur	153
Notes	167

Introduction

In my mind's eye, India is a kaleidoscope of every aspect of humanity. It is continually changing, colourful and complex. Culturally it radiates its influences globally through music, fashion and food. Philosophically its spirituality speaks to all, regardless of belief. The ancient Hindu Vedas and Buddhist scriptures touch base with what we know to be true of ourselves.

Since my mid-teens in the nineteen sixties, I had always wanted to visit India. The influence which Indian music and spirituality had on popular music and fashion at the time was profound. An exotic mix of Hindu mysticism, meditation and the use of Indian instruments such as the *sitar* and *tabla* drums, alongside the western guitar, contrasted radically and refreshingly with traditional rock and roll. This cultural shift shone a light on a country far more interesting than the UK in those drab post-war years.

Conversations over a glass or two of wine with my partner, friends and family, often led to discussions about holidays and trips abroad. Occasionally my desire to go to India would come up. 'Why India?' Was a question, which was often asked. At times, the question had a tinge of disapproval about it with comments reflecting preconceived ideas about the country and its people. Sometimes it was asked with what appeared to be a genuine sense of curiosity. This would lead me to wonder if there was some interest in someone joining me. I was looking for an 'India buddy', however none was to be found. If I were to go, it would have to be alone.

1. The Plan

In early 2019, while attending to family matters in a South Coast seaside town, I decided to get advice about single travel in India from a well-known high street travel agent. A friend who had used them on a number of occasions and was impressed with their skill at tailoring holidays according to individual wishes had recommended them to me.

I was excited as I entered the travel shop. After all, I had made my mind up that one way or another I would be going to India. This was my first step toward achieving that goal.

Telephones were ringing, photocopiers were humming and the opening and closing of filing cabinet drawers suggested that despite the digital age, paperwork was still an integral part of office life. The office was busy and I stood for a few expectant seconds looking to see if there was an expert available to guide me on my quest. There were several desks in the office, and each desk – with the exception of one by the shop front window – was occupied by an advisor speaking to customers, who, I noticed, were mainly couples. My wait was short-lived as a young man approached me and introduced himself as Rupert. He must have been about 23 years old judging by his fresh complexion, He was smartly turned out. The light grey suit he wore was complimented by a crisp white shirt and maroon tie. His well-polished black laced up shoes completed an image of confident efficiency. He reminded me of an estate agent, all smiles and cufflinks.

Rupert invited me to take a seat at the vacant desk by the window. He half listened, it seemed, to my ideas of solo travel in India. As we talked, I sensed I hadn't really engaged him. Perhaps it would have been different if I had had someone with me; a companion. He frequently glanced at his mobile phone laid in front of him on his desk, tapping its screen with an immaculately manicured nail, presumably to check why it had just buzzed or lit up. It was annoying and I felt myself becoming irritated and disappointed that full attention with a degree of enthusiasm was not being given to my trip of a lifetime.

"What about going on an elephant?" Rupert said flatly, as he craned his neck to look over my right shoulder to the window behind me facing the high street. I turned on my swivel chair to see what it was that was more interesting than my potential travel plans. Someone he knew was passing by. It was a young man walking slowly and giving one of those discreet waves, left hand with wriggling fingers raised just above hip level accompanied by a bashful smile. Turning back to face Rupert, I was in time to see him discreetly wave back.

Returning his gaze from the window, I noticed a slight blushing redness appearing around the front of Rupert's neck just above his immaculately tied collar. "Oh sorry," he said slightly flustered. "Where were we?" "Elephants," I said, in a dull, bemused tone, which was meant to be so.

Clearing his throat in two successive quiet little coughs, Rupert moved on from elephants and thumbed through a colourful brochure about travel in Southern Asia. After a while, as if he had solved the answer to a tricky cryptic crossword clue, he looked up at me from the brochure smiling and announced that I should see the Taj Mahal at sunrise, and take a toy train up the hillside. As the words left his lips, I was certain that he was aware of the unintended euphemism.

With an expression of mild embarrassment, eyes now wider than before, he licked his finger and sighed, and quickly turned the pages of the brochure. I did my best, but I'm sure he must have seen my face contort and my shoulders shake as I did my best to suppress a guffaw. It took a few minutes for me to settle down.

Suggestions were at last made about different combinations of travel arrangements such as taking iconic train journeys, and visiting old forts and temples. These would be well planned in advance and with guides or alone if I so wished.

This was a bit more like it, I thought; however, there were a couple of drawbacks. I didn't want to be committed to an itinerary, and the prices quoted were for two people. I explained this to Rupert and he assured me that he completely understood and would put something together and call me. He never called and I was neither surprised nor disappointed. The expertise and guidance I wanted was there I am sure, but it was not forthcoming.

It was clear that I alone would have to design, plan and execute this visit to India. In doing so, it was no longer a holiday, it was an adventure. I was nearing my 70th birthday and although healthy and brimming with confidence and self-belief, I was going to be travelling as an older person, alone and without the support of a guide or other travelling companions. I questioned the wisdom of my decision many times over in the coming months.

I thought for weeks about what and where I wanted to visit and how long I would need to stay. Initially, I had it in mind to visit some spiritual sites. My interest in Eastern philosophy had grown over the years. Varanasi with its colourful Hindu ceremonies beside the river Ganges; Lumbini, the birthplace of Buddha and Bodh Gaya, where it is said that he attained enlightenment, all called out to me.

I believe Rupert's suggestions referred to the tourist circuit of the Golden Triangle. New Delhi is at the triangles apex with Jaipur, the Pink City and Agra, home of the Taj Mahal, forming the triangles base. Although extremely interesting and apparently very beautiful, I had challenged myself to be a little more adventurous in my young old age. The tourist hot spots could wait a few more years.

After my enthusiasm for a more spiritual visit and considering the logistics of time and travel, I decided that my first trip to India required compromise. My initial travel ideas would have meant a lot of flying, but you can't see much of a country when you are flying at thirty thousand feet. Another important consideration was how much time I could negotiate away from home.

A month sounded like a very long time, although apparently that was about the average for travelling in India. Ten days was definitely too short. I thought three weeks sounded more realistic; however, I decided upon two weeks for a first attempt.

It occurred to me that rail travel would be a good way of seeing India, although I had some anxieties about it. I had seen films and videos of scores of people travelling on the top of overfull trains, many more holding onto the sides of carriages making their way along mountainside tracks skirting five-hundred-foot drops. I didn't intend travelling like that, but neither did I want to travel in the lap of luxury, waited upon British Raj style. I wanted a train journey that allowed me to travel with Indian people, speak to them and eat their food. I also wanted a seat by a window not too far from a toilet.

The toilet was important. What if I came down with a stomach bug and had diarrhoea and needed to vomit and couldn't get past the throngs of people to what may be an already occupied toilet? I reminded myself that thoughts were not facts. It helped for a while, but the whole scenario was played out in my head many times over in the coming months. At bedtime, India became a place of the mind. Before sleep, as my weary head settled into my pillow, the mystery of the journey ahead would unfold, as if revealed to me by a mystic, staring into the misty pond of my imagination. Despite the horrors unfolding in my mind, I decided that I would sit with my anxieties and fears, step outside of my comfort zone and travel by train anyway.

The next decision was where to travel. I bought a National Geographic adventure travel map of India. On one side was central and northern India. On the other side was southern India and Sri Lanka. India is huge; it was clear that without flying, I couldn't hope to travel further than the distance between two neat folds of my adventure map in the time allotted.

I decided to visit the south of the country. I had heard that the south was a gentler introduction to India for a first timer.

I chose Mumbai, the capital of the state of Maharashtra[1], as my initial point of arrival. My travel plan was developing.

The idea so far was to fly to Mumbai, stay for a couple of days and explore the city before travelling onwards.

After pouring over my map accompanied by a glass of red, and then another, my Indian adventure materialised before me like the enlightenment of Buddha. I would get a train from Mumbai and travel south 580 km further down the coast to Goa. I would stay in Goa for a few days then make my way 775 km south by train to Kochi in the state of Kerala[2]. The guidebooks describe Kerala's cities as being smaller than Mumbai and more relaxed. I was particularly interested in staying in Kochi with its port and atmospheric old quarters of Mattancherry and Fort Cochin.

Goa sounded lovely, stretching its laid-back self along 105 km of golden sands with a palm fringed coastline meeting the Arabian Sea – it sounded idyllic. Apparently, parts of Goa had quite a party culture, which I wanted to avoid as far as possible. My research led me to a fishing village in south Goa called Agonda. Agonda was described as having a beautiful beach with reasonable accommodation and local amenities. It sounded perfect.

The best time to visit southern India is between late October and April. The weather then is dry and hot but bearable with temperatures reaching around 32 degrees centigrade. From April to June, it can become uncomfortably hot. The monsoon season is from June through to September, which, I believe, can be depressingly wet. My plan was to go in mid-February 2020.

Having loosely planned my itinerary it was time to commit. There were plenty of airfare comparison sites which were easy to use and provided a wide range of options ranging from direct flights to flights with stopovers in various places, which, if time were not limited, would have been interesting and cheaper. I chose a direct flight from Heathrow to Mumbai with BA, which would be about 9 hours. I decided upon an evening departure from Heathrow on Sunday the 2nd of Feb 2020 returning from Mumbai late morning Sunday the 16th.

Booking the flight was easy. I paid extra for seat selection, choosing a window seat each way, by the emergency door. This gave me plenty of legroom for my left knee, which had recently become swollen and painful while trying to get back into running. A window was important as I looked forward to seeing the countries passing below me as I flew into the rising sun towards India.

It was now only April and I had another 10 months in which to plan my trip. I rested on my laurels for the next few months, however, I could now at least announce my departure date and discuss my itinerary with anyone who may be interested.

Summer came and went and with the arrival of October, I started to plan the rest of my trip. Having booked my flight to Mumbai I needed somewhere to stay. Online accommodation booking platforms were very useful. I was able to view loads of homestays, residencies, and hotels. Homestays are the equivalent of a B&B in the UK. Residencies are like hotels but smaller with less frills such as bar and restaurant. There was a wide range of prices and you could book without pre-payment or deposit, with a 48-hour cancellation option in most cases.

In my experience, the descriptions posted on the accommodation websites were pretty accurate. What you see on the site photographs is what you get. Comments left by guests and the star ratings which they gave all turned out to be accurate.

Mumbai is a big place and time for exploring was limited. I decided to stay in an area in south Mumbai called Fort. Fort is situated close to the more well-off, southern peninsula tourist area of Colaba. The accommodation I chose was within walking distance of the Chhatrapati Shivaji Terminus (CST), or more easily said Victoria train terminus. It was from here that I would depart for Goa.

My accommodation in Fort was a residency. It was rated by most of the web sites as three stars with mainly positive feedback. I had booked a double room for two nights at a total cost of Rs 9,492 or £106. You can visit India and live very cheaply if you wish. Accommodation can cost as little as a few pounds a night if you really need to be careful with your money. This type of accommodation will be very basic indeed. If you aim at a minimum of £30 each night you should be OK.

Communication with the residency through the booking website messaging service was good They arranged for a taxi to pick me up from the airport upon my arrival, which was reassuring.

One important consideration in planning this visit was medical help in the event of becoming unwell or having an accident. At the time of writing, I could access medical care pretty much anywhere in India as a tourist upon production of my visa.

Hospitals in India have variable standards. Private clinics and mission hospitals being preferable to state run ones. The big university hospitals are good and so are their facilities, but they often come at a price and payment can be asked for in advance for certain treatments. Government hospitals are generally free, however if you are an inpatient, you may need to find a 'friend' who will help with many basic nursing assistant services such as washing, eating and drinking. These services are missing in some of these hospitals. Some travel guide literature suggests paying a hospital cleaner or worker to become your 'friend'.

Thankfully, pharmacies sell most familiar medications without prescriptions and can offer advice for minor medical conditions. Many hotels have contact with a medical doctor, and most doctors in India speak English.

You are well covered medically in India from a medical science point of view; however, there are also Ayurvedic practitioners whose approach to health and well-being is more holistic. The Ayurvedic practitioner is concerned with restoring balance within the body. Herbal potions, and special diets may be prescribed along with yogic methods of physical and spiritual restoration. This ancient practice is over five thousand years old and is followed by millions in India and worldwide.

My next task was to think about the train journey to Goa, my accommodation there, and onward travel to Kochi. I had to get back to Mumbai as well for my return flight to London, so there was plenty to think about.

At the time of writing, train travel was really cheap in India and internal air travel was comparable to budget flights in the UK. My 12-hour train journey from Mumbai to Goa cost around £25 for an air-conditioned carriage. My return journey to Mumbai would be by air. A flight of about an hour cost around £60. I booked the train and my internal air tickets on line with a company called 12Go Asia. The process was easy and I would recommend the company.

There are no fewer than eight classes of train travel in India ranging from very basic second class to air-conditioned first. Second class, are mainly unreserved basic carriages with wooden seats and are often incredibly packed during the day. This class of carriage is best avoided for long travel.

The fare is so cheap for this class that it is virtually free. I chose AC2 travel. AC2 is an air-conditioned sleeper compartment for four people. The seats are bunk beds. The bottom two beds are used by all to sit on during the daytime. Each bed has a hygienic, comfortable plastic mattress.

I was able to reserve a bottom bunk and have the end next to the window. If you have a bottom bunk, you need to negotiate with whomever else is sitting on it if you wish to lie down. Pillows and bedding are provided free for each passenger even if it is a daytime journey. Other classes of travel are mainly air-conditioned and offer reasonable comfort.

First class AC1 is best with similar seating arrangements as AC2 but with carpets and relatively presentable bathrooms. AC1 prices are similar to an air-fare ticket.

My research into where to stay in Agonda, Goa, led me to charming but basic accommodation at a residency called 'My Friend's Place'. It was situated between forest and beach and was described as a restaurant, which had rooms with garden views. Google Earth was helpful in having a bird's eye view of Agonda and location of the accommodation. It looked to be ideally situated and the accommodation, although simple, was just what I wanted.

India is complex politically and socially. It is important to note this when planning a visit. Unrest had been growing in India since December 2019 when the Indian parliament passed the Citizen (Amendment) Act 2019. The act served to fast track Indian citizenship for persecuted religious minority groups who had entered India prior to 2015. The minority groups were specifically from Afghanistan, Bangladesh and Pakistan. The religious groups identified did not include Muslims. The exclusion of Muslims was seen as discriminatory and attracted global criticism. In India, there were nationwide demonstrations and rallies represented by those for and against the act. Frequent clashes between the two combined with violent police intervention resulted in a number of deaths and many injuries and arrests. At the time of writing, the Indian government have downplayed the significance of the act. Many administrative areas in India have not implemented it.

I decided to sign up to the *gov.uk* daily report. The *gov.uk* site is useful for general travel abroad giving advice and guidance on visa applications, contact information for embassies, travel advice for specific countries and much more. Each morning I would update myself by visiting the site and they would email me about new developments.

Occasionally, *gov.uk* would highlight the unrest in India and advise against travel to countries such as Bangladesh or certain areas of Delhi. There were no warnings issued for Mumbai or Kochi.

Indian politics and social unrest were soon to make way for a much greater challenge. There was a case of the Covid-19 virus in Kerala which had infected two people. The *gov.uk* site didn't issue any advice on this at the time though it was being reported in the news.

This virus would, as everyone now knows, change the world, and in particular, India. As I write, India has suffered dreadfully with over 31.4 million cases and 421 thousand deaths.

Reports of the virus in China were already appearing on our television screens at home and pretty much everyone was aware of it.

We knew it was serious in China, however the expectation was that it would remain there and be contained. The fact that it had appeared in Kerala was something of a surprise. It helped me to make a decision not to go there. I wasn't feeling completely comfortable about going in the first place. It felt like I was cramming too much into two weeks. I would go no further south than Goa.

The days and weeks passed. Xmas came, then New Year. It was now time to apply for my visa, which could not be done sooner than 30 days before the intended date of arrival in India. This was a lengthy online process via a link on the *gov.uk* website. I received an approval email only a few days after my application and printed off two copies of the visa.

Photographs are required when applying for an Indian entry visa. The specifications for the size and requirements of the photos are different to those for a UK passport. I found a passport photo booth that produced official visa photographs for India and UK passports.

Having booked travel and accommodation I was now ready to attend to the practical stuff. I bought a rucksack, insect repellent, insect and mosquito bite remedy, sterile hand wipes and gel, Imodium and high factor sun lotion. For Xmas,

I had an invaluable joint gift from the family. It is called a Life Straw and it is a water bottle with a filter in it, which will filter water from pretty much any source to a purity of 99.9%. This bottle did two things: first, it meant I could safely drink ordinary tap water from any tap in India, and secondly, it also meant I never had to buy plastic bottles of water and thus add to the enormous mountain of plastic bottles produced by visitors like me every day of every year in India. This magic bottle helped to ensure that I remained well-hydrated and never had an upset stomach.

I kept clothes to a minimum, ensuring an adequate supply of underwear and socks. A friend of mine was going on a tour of Europe with her fiancé in a campervan at about the same time as my adventure. She told me about some underpants, which she had bought which didn't need changing for about 6 weeks. Apparently, they self cleaned. I believe it may have been one of those inventions that came out of the NASA space programme.

It was an interesting prospect. Apparently, they cost about £26 a pair. It amused me to think of how well they would cope in India. Someone suggested that if I kept the receipts and labels, I may be able to return them when I got back if they weren't up to the job.

I packed two of pairs of shorts, four t-shirts and a pair of jeans. I was sure I would be able to do a bit of personal washing along the way. My wash-bag contained a stick deodorant shaving gel and a razor. My toothpaste was a small tube and my toothbrush and interdental brushes were new. I figured that if shower gel wasn't available at my various accommodations, I would use shaving gel. Most importantly,

I packed my straw Panama style hat to protect my baldhead from the sun.

With my rucksack packed and important documents and essential equipment such as phone charger, earphones, Life Straw, glasses and wallet set aside for carrying in my manbag, I was ready.

2. Cometh the Hour

The 2nd of February arrived. I woke up that grey cold morning after a fitful sleep to the realisation that I was about to embark on an adventure which had been discussed, swept under the carpet then resurrected over a glass of wine many times over the past several years. The poor sleep seemed to have affected my left knee pain. I had been struggling with it since just before Xmas and it was to plague me throughout the next two weeks. This morning it was tender and swollen.

Having given careful consideration to what clothes I should wear on my journey, I decided upon my light-coloured Chino trousers, which, in retrospect, was not the brightest idea for a long-haul flight for reasons that will become clear. A short sleeve shirt and a fleece top with the option of a hooded zip-up fleece provided a degree of flexibility in the event of temperature changes. I would carry the hooded top with me in my manbag. Trainers were the only footwear I would have for the entire trip. The idea was to be warm in the UK and shed clothes as necessary when I got to India.

The other idea was that if I turned up for my flight reasonably dressed, I might be in with a chance of an upgrade.

My flight was scheduled for 8.45pm. I wanted to give myself an hour and a half at least in the complimentary lounge, which I was entitled to use courtesy of a deal I had with my travel insurance.

I decided to get to Heathrow terminal 5 at around 3.30pm. This left me plenty of time after check-in to relax with a glass or two of beer and a light bite to get me into the zone before making my way to the departure gate.

I had been offered a lift to Heathrow by my friends, Al and Chris. My lift arrived just before 2 pm. I recall the feeling of excitement upon hearing the knock on the front door. Opening it, I was greeted by a widely smiling Al who immediately launched into his often-heard Indian person speaking English accent. Whenever my trip to India came up, he couldn't help but revert to his Peter Sellers 'goodness gracious me' impersonation.

The journey from Fareham in Hampshire of just over an hour was made short by conversation. Chris and my partner Carol nattered away in the back, while Al and I talked about the trip ahead. Excitement and anticipation grew as the miles ticked by. It seemed that it was no time at all before we were leaving the M25 and the Heathrow signs had appeared. Terminal 5 signs soon followed.

Getting out of the car and feeling the cold air hitting my nostrils and cheeks, I tuned into those unmistakeable airport sounds and smells. Even if you were blindfold you would have known where you were. A distant female announcement, preceded by the sound of 'bing-bong', announced something about passengers on some flight or another followed by another voice announcing security advice.

Baggage trolleys clattering as passengers loaded their over-packed suitcases before embracing their lifts with farewells or thanking taxi drivers. Mixed with the cold early

February air, the smell of kerosene from the jet exhausts of aircraft arriving and departing from the terminal and the whining of their turbines added to the excitement.

I said goodbye to Carol, and as usual, she was smiling and reassuring. I shook Al's hand thanking him for the lift. He returned my thanks with "you are very, very, welcome" in that Peter Sellers Indian accent. I waved at Chris, who stayed in the back of the car due to mobility issues. The car pulled away and waves were exchanged until they were out of sight. No one wanted to be the first to stop waving.

Check-in was easy. I was first in the queue and the check-in lady was pleasant and efficient. I had my boarding pass on my phone, which made me feel like I was right up there with technology. I even had my complimentary lounge pass on it. It felt strange allowing my rucksack to be taken from me. My whole means of living was in it and as it began its jerky journey along the conveyor belt I remember thinking I wouldn't see it again until my arrival in Mumbai. My only possessions were now in my manbag which was slung securely around my neck.

For those who remember air travel before the terrible attacks on the World Trade Centre in 2001, it may be agreed that the experience is no longer the special occasion it used to be. Following the day of those attacks, which would later be known universally as 9/11, the glamorous side of air travel changed quite literally overnight. I recall having arrived in Cyprus several days before 9/11, on a very good flight from Gatwick for a ten-day holiday with Carol and two friends. On our flight there, we were looked after by smiling, laid-back, cabin crew. It was a great start to our holiday. The return flight to the UK was very different.

Flying is a serious affair now – and quite rightly. I find going through security, an uncomfortable, sometimes stressful experience. There is the potential of getting it wrong and being told off. You need to wake up from your holiday daydreaming for a while and pay attention. "Stop there and wait please." "OK step forward, shoes off, belt off, all items in the tray." "Jacket please." It calls to mind a prisoner arriving at the custody suite receiving instructions prior to being banged up. Indeed I always feel relieved and a sense of achievement like passing a test once my personal belongings appear again after having disappeared on the conveyor belt through the rubber strips of the scanning machine. God help you if you have had a knee or hip replacement or both.

Chris set the alarm off on the scanner, every time we took our annual trip to the sun with her and Al. She was often subjected to a thorough frisking but I never heard her complain.

Following the rigours of security the relaxed atmosphere of the shopping area was like a reward. The aromas and colours of ladies perfume displays mingling with aftershaves and men's grooming products lent an air of sensual opulence to the moment. Duty free spirits with special whiskies and brandies, golden in their pristine glass bottles, did a good job of saying 'buy me'.

The heady mixture of perfumes was gradually replaced by the many restaurants, coming into view offering something for every taste. They were welcoming and busy with customers passing the time before their flight to somewhere in the world. Like me, they would be weary and bedraggled when they reached their destination. I wondered where each of them was going and what their story was. It was a special time.

It was now about 4:30pm and I headed for the complimentary lounge. This was an important stage of my journey. It was to here that my imagination took me most nights, mentally rehearsing the start of a journey not yet made.

The two ladies at the lounge reception desk looked Pilipino, which gave things an eastern feel. Smiling widely, I proudly produced my complimentary lounge pass on my phone. They returned my smile with their own no doubt well-rehearsed welcome.

The lounge looked comfortable and inviting. There was a self-service food servery, which had a good choice of hot and cold foods and a well-stocked bar with an extensive range of spirits, liquors, beers, lagers and wines. Food and drink were all inclusive.

The seating in the lounge was well thought out and seemed to be geared towards the single passenger as well as groups and couples. Finding myself in a little self-contained, crescent shaped pod with room for little more than one person and their hand baggage I made myself at home. There were two electrical sockets, a lamp and a small table. The seat was comfortable and the semi-enclosed pod gave a degree of privacy. I immediately made myself at home. Unpacking my manbag, I plugged my phone into its charger and put my earphones on charge ready for the journey. Whatever lay ahead, music would accompany me.

Asking for a lager and returning to my pod I drank and got into that relaxed, dreamy frame of mind that comes with a first holiday drink. The lager was cool, refreshing and comforting after the tense atmosphere of security. Following another lager it was time to eat. The self-service food counter offered a reasonable choice of meat and vegetarian dishes. My choice was vegetarian curry. I then remembered that I had ordered the Asian selection for my meals on board the flight as well. Ah well… *When in India,* I thought.

The time went by well enough. There was a wall-mounted television ahead of me. The sound was off but it was tuned into the BBC news channel. I noticed that every so often the breaking news panel at the bottom of the screen would show snippets of the latest numbers of infections and deaths of the Covid-19 outbreak in Wuhan city, China. By now, just about everyone was aware of this virus. The world was watching.

6 pm came around and I decided to move on towards the gate. With the help of those beers, I was now in the right frame of mind. The alcohol, along with some paracetamol which I had taken when I arrived at the lounge, made my knee feel considerably better too. It had been bothering me for most of the day.

Following the signs to the gate and not in a hurry, I passed a welcoming bar and decided to have just one more lager. It went down a treat and I was now in gear.

The route to the gate wasn't as straightforward as I thought it would be. There was quite a long walk before catching a shuttle train. The trains were frequent which is just as well since there were quite a few people making their way to their gates. I noticed that every time a train arrived, a cleaner would wipe all surfaces down before the doors would open and allow passengers to board. This delayed things a little.

Upon boarding, it was standing room only. By now, my bladder, which had not been emptied since the complimentary lounge, filled fast. Without warning, I was in one of those bladder-bursting situations, which for men is truly a sweat inducing moment of terror. To make things worse I was wearing the light-coloured Chinos, which are unforgiving even for a minute dribble. It was mind wrecking, relentless torture. The ride was quite fast; however, at the peak of my desperation, to my horror the next stop was not mine.

The shuttle slowly and painfully came to a halt to drop off passengers for their terminal. *Breathe,* I thought as I tried not to feed into the sensations with thoughts of going. Just allow yourself to relax. It helped a bit as we started off again; however, it wasn't long before the sensations returned. By now, I felt my face flushing and I was beginning to do a little dance, which was nothing more than alternate, heal raises and undetectable pelvic squeezes. It felt longer, but after a minute or two we arrived at the stop for my gate. Rushing off of the shuttle, which stirred up the discomfort in my knee, I could see a toilet ahead. I ran praying that it wasn't being cleaned or was out of order for some reason. To my relief, It was not. I was greeted by several pristine urinals arranged in a row and to my delight none were occupied. Quickly choosing the nearest urinal, I allowed my manbag to drop from my shoulders to the floor and unzipped. That moment of physical and emotional release was terrific.

There is a peculiarity that when men of a certain age have finished going for a pee and having just shaken the last drops off, tucked themselves in and done themselves up, there can still be 10 ml left in the pipework. As with all water this will take the path of least resistance, which for me was down my left leg just below the crutch. When in your own home this is not such a problem, however, when out in public it can be somewhat embarrassing. If I had been wearing jeans, it probably would have gone unnoticed but I was wearing cream chinos and the 10 ml went a long way.

There was only one thing for it. I went to the sink to wash my hands and made splashes over the front of my chinos to make it look like I had had a sink accident. Feeling confident, I left the toilets and made my way to the gate.

The gate area was crowded. Many of the passengers looked Asian – probably British Indians, I imagined, visiting family in India. Some looked quite elderly. Many of the older women wore traditional *saris* while the younger ones dressed informally, mostly in Jeans. The men accompanying them looked like they had made an effort to be smart as some of them, particularly the older ones, were wearing suits. A few children, and some babes in arms already looked restless and I wondered how they were going to cope with a nine-hour flight.

It was now under an hour before our take off and I was excited. Any minute now the announcement would be made for passengers to approach the gate for boarding. Then it came. "For passengers of BA199 we regret to inform you that there will be a delay of approximately 20 mins due to a technical problem."

Oh well, I thought, these things happen. 25 minutes later, another announcement came. "For passengers of flight BA199 we regret that unfortunately due to a continuing technical issue we advise every passenger with prior arranged airport lounge facilities to return to them and await further information. For all others please be seated and we will keep you informed."

This was not what I wanted. Well, of course, neither did anyone else, but after all, this was my India adventure and I didn't want anything to go wrong. If only I had packed that crystal ball in my manbag. If I had I would have been able to navigate my way through what was to follow much more smoothly.

I decided to return to the complimentary lounge, which meant making my way back to departures. I asked someone at an information desk how to get back. He told me to take the stairs down to level 1 and follow the signs to departures. I went downstairs to level 1 and, through a door saying, 'To Departures'. I walked for ages. The man at the information desk had sent me on a walk through a tunnel, which was parallel to the shuttle train tunnel that I had previously been on. Presumably, he would have suggested taking the train back if it was possible to do so, instead of making me walk.

I hardly saw a soul for the entire walk which must have been at least three-quarters of a mile. The tunnel was dimly lit and the occasional maintenance man on a little motorised trolley with an orange flashing light on the top of a pole just above his head would pass me beeping his horn as though to say I shouldn't be there. Thinking about it, I probably shouldn't have. It was probably a maintenance or service tunnel. At last, there it was, the sign above a door saying 'Departures'. I was relieved. My knee was now swollen and very sore. I was sweating buckets after my long and, what turned out to be, unnecessary walk underground.

It had been so quiet in the tunnel apart from the distant rumble of what must have been the shuttle train on the other side of the wall. Pushing my way through the exit door into the main departures lounge, a sudden rush of noise and light met my senses; people going to and fro, announcements, and the clatter of trolleys transporting passengers and baggage. Neon signs advertising airlines, expensive watches and exotic destinations dazzled me momentarily.

There was an information desk by the door I had just come through. The lady in attendance was in her mid-forties by the look of her. She had a matronly air about her and looked slightly stern and authoritative. Her neatly arranged collar length nut-brown hair, complimented a smart blue suit with red neck scarf, which was immaculately arranged over a crisp white blouse reflecting confident professionalism. I approached her reverently and asked in which direction the complimentary lounge was. It must have been obvious to her that I was flustered although for what reason she was, at this point, unaware. She smiled neutrally and indicated precisely in which direction I should walk. I thanked her, but just before turning to go on my way I asked if there was any further information about my delayed flight number BA199. "Oh my goodness!" she said with a frown and an expression close to a telling off, "you should return immediately to the boarding gate, didn't you hear the announcement?" That did it really, I had had enough. My face no doubt reddening and eyes widening with each sentence I launched into a pointless frustrated monologue. "No, I didn't hear the announcement, because I was sent by one of your colleagues, on a very long and probably unnecessary underground walk, to return to my complimentary lounge which was suggested I do, and there were no announcements down there." All of this without drawing a breath and my voice emphasising the word 'there'. She looked at me with one of those, 'this person is being aggressive towards me', and 'maybe I should call security' looks. Realising that I was beginning to act like an angry ass, I quickly backtracked. "It doesn't matter," I said sharply, "which way is the shuttle please?" Without making further eye contact, and without speaking, with mouth slightly twisted in distaste, she raised her right arm and pointed in a general direction. "Thank you," I said, intentionally lowering my frustrated voice in in an attempt to demonstrate emotional control had returned.

Being told to get a move on, my frustration gave way to anxiety and panic for fear of hearing an announcement naming me as the person now holding up the departure of flight BA199. "Final call for passenger so and so," the one we hear when we are going on holiday. The one where we smile at one another with expressions of judgemental disbelief, shaking our heads and asking each other, "Well, how the hell can that ever happen? Some people are just unbelievable."

After hobbling for only a few minutes, I was able to board the shuttle, and this time, without incident, I arrived at the gate departures platform for my flight. My heart was racing and my knee, which now aching and swollen again was, beginning to get me down as I boarded the escalator for the departures gate level.

All passengers expecting to board were waiting as requested by the announcement, which I had not heard. Restless children were whining, it was way past their bedtime. A few were lying on the floor splayed out, restless fighting sleep. The older passengers sat composed and accepting while the younger ones especially the men were showing signs of agitation, gesticulating to one another occasionally raising their voices above normal speech level. Then it came, "Passengers for flight BA199 are regrettably informed that the flight is cancelled. Please wait for further information regarding a reschedule."

The straw, for breaking the camel's back had arrived. It was all going wrong. It wasn't meant to be like this and I was close to abandoning the trip.

More information came in the form of a text message on my phone telling me that the next available flight would be in 24 hours and asking me to please acknowledge acceptance by clicking on the link.

I clicked on the link and shortly afterwards I received another text message telling me that I had been booked on the 8:45am flight the next day. This meant a delay of 12 not 24 hours, which was at least some good news.

Further announcements were made. We were all to make our way to the arrivals hall, collect our luggage and board a coach, which would take us to a hotel for the night. It was now 10:45 and with a 05:45am check-in. I would have to set my alarm very early indeed in order to allow time to get back to the departures lounge from whatever hotel it was that I was to be billeted. I had no idea how far away this hotel was.

I joined the procession of disgruntled passengers being led back to the arrivals hall to collect the off-loaded luggage. I felt sorry for the parents, grandparents and crying children being carried by weary mothers. They would be transported to some unknown location to rest their heads for the remainder of the night. I, on the other hand, had decided that I would settle down somewhere in departures to rest my head for the few hours remaining to check in.

Standing at the carousel watching the bags going around was demoralising. Normally the carousel experience is accompanied by a sense of arrival and an end to travel.

Passengers wearily snatched their luggage from the broad, black belt as it made its way on its circular journey. Luggage retrieved, they were shepherded out to their allocated coaches for transportation to their allocated hotel. It was now past midnight as the last passengers left the area. I found myself standing alone staring at an empty carousel. My rucksack had failed to turn up. There were a few unclaimed bags lying around on the floor. I looked over them but my rucksack just wasn't there. The few beers I had drunk earlier had now worn off, leaving me slightly hung-over, tired and thirsty. *God,* I thought, *what now?*

A very pleasant airport assistant, smartly dressed in her BA uniform, who had been assisting and directing my fellow passengers to their coach approached me. She said the final coach to a hotel would be leaving shortly. I explained that I would not be getting on it. I wasn't going to leave without finding out where my rucksack was. Once I had located it, I would sleep wherever I could in the airport.

The lady looked at me with concern and asked me if I was quite sure that I wanted to do this. I explained as calmly and as politely as was possible under the circumstances that by the time I got into bed at whatever hotel I was being taken to, it would no doubt be time to get up and come back to the airport for my check-in, 3 hours before departure. She smiled and agreed that I had a point and proceeded to help me find my bag. Looking more closely at the few pieces of luggage, which, for some unknown reason, hadn't been claimed I saw a child's car seat with something underneath it – my luggage. My rucksack sat almost undetectable under the upturned seat. It was only the familiar ribbon, which I had attached to the rucksack for easy recognition that was visible. I felt a rush of relief as I picked it up and flung it over my shoulder.

3. To Sleep Perchance to Dream

It was just me, my rucksack and the helpful lady left in the arrivals hall. The hall was silent except for the distant hum of a cleaner running a machine over the floor at the other end of the hall near the toilets. Smiling with calm professionalism, even now at 1 am, the lady led me to a computer terminal nearby and switched it on.

"Let's get you checked in now and see if we can find a nice seat," she said with great compassion.

"But I have a seat, I paid extra for it," I replied.

"I'm afraid that won't be possible for this trip but you will get the seat you paid for upon your return," she said.

The seat, which I had paid for was pivotal to my enjoyment of the flight to India. *Another disappointment*, I thought, by now feeling tired and low.

"You will have to put in a claim for your seat," the lady said.

Feeling beaten I said "OK," my voice dropping a tone. I was glad the lady didn't turn out to be the one at the enquiries desk earlier that evening.

She checked me into a window seat, which I was grateful for. She gave me my boarding pass, and with a concerned smile handed me a voucher for some food and drink to a value of 10 pounds.

"Now what will you do?" she said. I said I would try to find somewhere to sleep. She suggested Costa Coffee upstairs one level. She said that I might be able to doze in one of their chairs. She smiled and elegantly walked off. A guardian angel, never to be seen again.

At Costa Coffee, apart from the two staff members there was a young man laying on a bench seat, which made a perfect bed and an older looking man at a small table, eyes closed, resting his head on his folded arms. Both looked as if they had come in to take shelter from the cold for the night. I was envious of the man on the bench seat as there weren't any others to be seen. I did manage to put two dining seats together with the intention of lying down. I made myself as comfortable as possible. Putting on my jacket because I was now cold, I pulled up the hood on my woollen zip top and tried to get into a foetal position. Lying flat was useless since the gap between the two chairs dug into my back. The café wasn't far from automatic doors, which led outside to the arrivals pick-up area. Each time they opened they let in the cold February early morning air. They did this every time someone went near them which was pretty much constantly with cleaners and staff coming on and going off shifts.

The bright lights of the café bothered me too, even with my eyes closed, so I put on my sunglasses. I thought I must have looked a sight so I took a selfie out of boredom. I did look a sight. I remember thinking that I wouldn't want to meet myself in a dark alleyway. Looking around at the others staying the night at the café I felt I was in good company.

I tried to sleep but had no success. Music was playing and the kitchen staff kept banging their filter coffee spoons on their machines to get rid of the drags. I think they were doing it on purpose because no one was buying anything as far as I could see.

I decided to move and look around for somewhere quieter and more comfortable. I hadn't noticed before that at the other end of the café seating area – away from the automatic doors and just out of sight of the café itself – there was one bench. I thought it might be possible to stretch out on it and get some sleep. It felt reasonably comfortable so I established myself there, placing my rucksack under my head as a pillow and curling up with my back against the lights. For a while, I felt sleep coming, then annoyingly I got the urge to pee. It's no good trying to sleep when you need to empty your bladder. You just drift in and out of waves of urgency. Annoyed but glad that at least I had somewhere to get my head down for a while, I gathered my Rucksack and manbag together and walked to the far end of the building to the toilets.

I was pleased to think that I had used another 15 minutes of time and was moving closer to check in, which was now about three and a half hours away. Feeling more comfortable having used the toilet, I made my way back to my bench seat. I was now really quite desperate to sleep. My pace quickened, but as I approached the café my heart sank as I arrived at the seating area to find my bench seat taken. I felt a great injustice had been done to me. I wanted to tell the person that my need for sleep was urgent and that I had seen it first. But then, looking at her, it was plain to see that she was homeless, surrounded by all those signs of homelessness; plastic bags full of her belongings and one dirty looking rucksack. I reminded myself of the short discomfort I was experiencing now and the prospect of a warm aircraft cabin later, with hot meals, red wine and a movie or two. This lady had no such prospects, but I remember thinking that perhaps she still had hope. I silently wished her well and left her to her dreams.

It was hopeless and there was no chance of sleep now with only 3 hours before check in. I wandered around departures making the occasional trip to the toilet, each time splashing my face with water in an attempt to sharpen up. I remembered the voucher I had been given and bought a coffee and pastry from the café, which gave me a momentary boost of energy before sliding back into weariness. The next couple of hours passed slowly, but increasingly there was more to see and distract me. The trickle of people coming through those accursed doors increased and the airport began to come to life again.

At last, it was now 5:30 am and re-energised at the thought of a warm breakfast in the complimentary lounge which opened at 5 am, I shook off my fatigue and made my way to the BA check in. Not surprisingly I was first there. The check-in hadn't opened yet but staff were beginning to take their stations. Eventually, my check in opened and handing over my rucksack once more to the operator I said goodbye to it and made my way to security, which was more relaxed this time with only a handful of passengers going through.

The perfume and duty-free shops were quiet now. There were no sales assistants, just a cleaner here and there. The air of luxury and opulence experienced the previous afternoon had of course been an illusion created by the staff and the theatre they crafted.

I made my way eagerly to the complimentary lounge passing the restaurants, which were now closed with the exception of one small coffee shop. The lounge was warm and inviting. There were no other customers, and the pod I had used at my last visit was vacant. I immediately made myself at home in that cosy little space. After the experiences of the last several hours, it felt like heaven. A hot breakfast was on offer. I had scrambled eggs on toast with mushrooms on the side with baked beans and a mug of sweet tea. I ate enthusiastically, savouring the satisfying warmth that hot food can bring when tired and hungry. Relaxing on the soft cushion-backed seat, I reflected on the farce, which had unfolded since arriving at the boarding gate the previous evening. With the intention of closing my eyes very briefly, sleep must have come quickly.

"Excuse me sir, excuse me," a hand on my shoulder gently shaking me. Coming too from what must have been a very deep sleep I was being woken by the receptionist who had logged my arrival. She heard the call for my name announcing last call to the gate. Having confirmed that she had woken the right person, she phoned the gate to tell them I was found. "You must hurry sir, they will wait for only 20 minutes more." Collecting my belongings, and in a state of panic I ran through the departures terminal like a shoplifter who had just been rumbled. My heart pounded and I was breathing hard as I got to the shuttle train with a feeling of utter helplessness in the face of time. The shuttle arrived, coming slowly to a stop. Waiting for a cleaner to wipe all surfaces before allowing me, the only passenger to board, was excruciating. I now only had 15 minutes to get to the gate. It took 10 minutes to arrive at my destination and with only 5 minutes left, my now very painful knee didn't stop me from sprinting up the escalator. I couldn't stand there waiting for it to trundle to the top.

The waiting gate staff saw me running towards them. One was waving her hands motioning me to hurry. She reminded me of one of those marshals at the London Marathon who shout 'come on, you can do it, well done' and as you get there puts a finishers medal over your head. Embarrassed, in pain with my knee, and fumbling for my passport and boarding card I was politely invited to hurry along to the waiting aircraft, which was about to close its door. Again, I hurried along almost dragging my painful leg now as I made my way through the boarding tunnel. Arriving at the aircraft door, red faced and full of apologies, I was greeted with what was no doubt a mandatory well-practiced smile for the likes of me.

My boarding pass was checked and I was directed to my seat. I heard the aircraft door close with a thump. My tired paranoid mind told me it might have been slammed out of frustration. Making my way through the cabin trying to find my seat I felt as if all eyes were on me. Despite my embarrassed smiles no one else was smiling, just looking.

The small Indian family of three, were settled in their seats, belts fastened with their 18-month-old daughter sleeping peacefully in its mothers arms. Red faced from exertion, pain and embarrassment, I apologetically asked if I could get to my seat, which, as arranged by the helpful lady earlier that morning, was a window seat. They were pleasant and showed no irritation as first the rather plump father stood after unbuckling his seat, followed by the equally plump mother with chubby, sleeping child in arms. I slid past them with a squeeze and sat down with a bump. Quickly fastening my seat belt and preparing myself for the 9 hours ahead I gave a grateful look towards the young family whose peace I had just disturbed and let out a deep sigh of relief. It was good to take the weight off of my knee, which was now very tender and throbbed. I recalled my thoughts last night when I poured scorn on those people who for some reason or another don't get to the gate on time. "How the hell do they do that? unbelievable!"

The child began to wake. I felt sure that my late arrival had undone the mother's work in getting her off to sleep. She began to scream and it was shrill. The mother gently shook her in her cradled arms hoping to get her to drop back off to sleep again but the child fought the attempts and wriggled and squirmed and screamed even louder, sometimes it seemed, turning almost blue beneath her dark Indian complexion. I thought that perhaps she might settle once we started to move off. Then came an announcement, which was difficult to hear over the screaming child. "Good morning ladies and gentlemen, this is the captain." He announced a delay of about 20 minutes due to a passenger no longer being able to take the flight. It would take a little while to off-load them. I could have joined the child in a screaming contest. It was interesting to note that I suddenly felt vindicated and no longer the bad guy. Suddenly the judged became judgemental and all sorts of pictures about this person and the sort of human being they must be came to mind. A voice in my head reminded me that I had no idea about their circumstances and that I should shut up, so I did.

How many more difficulties would I have to endure before getting to India? I thought. Mercifully the 20 minutes became 15 with the announcement that the issue had been resolved and that we were ready to push back and taxi for take off. The child was now on full throttle. The mother was getting distressed, apologising to me frequently and close to tears by the look of her. An air-hostess leaned across her and asked me if I would like to move to a seat at the rear of the aircraft away from the noise. I said, "No, thank you, I have children of my own, I am used to it." The hostess smiled, nodded and went away. I had sat in the back of an aircraft on my way from Tenerife to the UK. It was cramped and there was no window.

The mother, hearing my reply used it, I suppose, as a way of communicating with me. "You have children also," she said shouting over the child's screams and the rumble of the taxiing aircraft. Her voice juddering as she gently shook the child in an attempt to calm it. "How old are they?" she asked, continuing to shake the baby. "47 and 50," I said, thinking it would be hilarious. "Oh," she said with a straight face, and that was the end of the conversation.

Looking out of the window meant turning my head away from the screaming child, which was a relief. Surely, she couldn't sustain that level of energy expenditure for 9 hours, I thought. Despite the commotion, I started to settle down and enjoyed the take off which I have always loved. The engines opened up, and the acceleration pulled me back in my seat as we raced down the runway. Soon I felt the sensation of gravity pulling at me as the aircraft left the tarmac and we climbed steadily towards cruising height. I remember looking down on London. It was a Monday morning and I thought about all those people at work and tourists from all over the world about to start an exhausting day of sightseeing around the capital. The child seemed to like the take off as well, as there was a gradual throttling back of the screaming and by the time we had reached the top of our climb she had levelled off and was happily playing with a paper bag.

It seemed that in no time we had left the coast of England and were well over France heading down to Italy. The next few hours passed by easily enough. I used the time to accustom myself to my tiny space.

Approaching lunchtime a steward came around with the drinks trolley and nibbles, which were all included in the airfare. Dressed in his BA cabin staff uniform he had an air of professional efficiency about him. He was clearly enjoying his job, smiling and laughing with passengers as he approached my row of seats. "Any drinks here?" he said smiling. "Yes please," I said eagerly. I asked if I could have a red wine as an aperitif and another for my meal. "Of course," he said looking a little concerned, "but how about two bottles before and two during?" *This is how my adventure should start,* I thought. As he handed me the four bottles, I experienced indescribable happiness. After all the cruelty life had poured on me over the last 24 hours this was heaven.

The practicalities of lunch amused me. The table was hardly big enough for my tray of food let alone my four bottles of wine, which I stored in various places. One down the side of my seat, two in that net thing on the back of the seat in the front that has the inflight information and magazines. The little family next to me were in the same position but they had their daughter too – who was now sleeping – to juggle between them. The usual pattern of long-haul activities unfolded. Wine followed by lunch, then a snooze followed by a film, another snooze, then for this flight, an evening meal.

The journey was interesting and I was able to track my progress on the in-flight entertainment screen in front of me.

Unfortunately we were flying into darkness which was disappointing as my original plan was to see the sun rising and observe the land below as we flew east. However, with the aid of the in-flight information displayed on the entertainment screen in front of me I was able to track our progress as it grew darker around five hours into our flight.

I was able to see the lights of countries as we passed over them and of particular interested was the glow of towns below me as we passed over parts of Afghanistan and Pakistan. They were places of secrecy, potentially unsafe for westerners we have been led to believe. I wondered what the truth of the matter really was as we passed over them edging ever closer to our destination.

We were now 45 minutes from Mumbai. The cabin became busy with crew tidying up and people beginning to pack their things away in preparation for landing. Looking out at the night sky I could make out the growing glow of Mumbai. The closer we got the more evident was the immense thick looking blanket of smog, which enveloped the area. It was clear that the city air was significantly polluted, as at the edges it looked relatively starry and clear in the night sky. Turning now and a little bumpy with turbulence we came into position on finals. The descent seemed to go on forever. The aircraft engines rising and falling in pitch as the pilot made adjustments to speed and height. Then, quite suddenly it seemed, I could see streams of traffic below me as we broke through the cloud and pollution and made our final lunge towards the runway. The wheels made contact quite smoothly followed by the roar of reverse thrust as the aircraft began its breaking and deceleration before coming to taxy speed. I was in India. I had arrived.

4. India

As the door of the aircraft cabin opened, there was a gradual rise in temperature from a comfortable 20 degrees Celsius to somewhere around 30 degrees. The aroma of the warm Indian night air mingled with familiar airport smells began to meet my nostrils as if to say: "Hello, welcome to India."

Shuffling along the cabin isle as I moved closer to the exit, I remember being surprised at the freshness and energy of the cabin crew bidding farewell to their payload of weary travellers.

Making my way to arrivals, I followed the rest of the passengers who appeared to be mainly Indian and seemed to know what to do. The international arrivals terminal was big. Inaugurated in 2014 the architects and designers had done a great job. The long, very wide walkway from the aircraft to immigration was opulently carpeted with a peacock feather eye design in yellow, purples and white. The lighting was bright but not uncomfortable. Every 30 metres or so, there were wall panels depicting mythical, historical and contemporary India. The long walk was mercifully interspersed at regular intervals with moving walkways, although it did my knee good to get some exercise after sitting for so long.

Finally, arriving at the main immigration hall, passengers began forming lines in front of the manned entry cubicles. I saw a sign saying E-visas I so joined that. It was a long queue and there must have been a hundred or more passengers waiting to have their entry documents checked by just four officials. Just as I was starting to get a bit despondent, a shout went out from a tubby moustachioed official in a khaki uniform. "E-visas from the UK queue at isle 7." I could see that there were only about 40 people already there so I put on a spurt and made it pretty much at 41st position before the rest of the passengers with E-visas got their stuff together and joined the dash.

Looking behind me the queue was now quickly building and began to snake back all along the hall to where I had entered it. I was so glad that I had got to where I was, for the whole process of immigration was painfully slow. I had arranged for my taxi to pick me up at 9 pm. It was now around midnight. I phoned the residency and spoke to the very helpful night porter to explain about the delay. He told me not to worry and assured me that the driver would be happy to wait. I couldn't imagine how that could be; however, I was grateful for the reassurance. Looking at the snail's pace ahead of me for processing entry it was going to be at least another two hours.

Slowly, very slowly, each passenger next in line was called forward to the only E-visa check-in open. The routine was to hand in your passport and disembarkation document, then your visa. If all was in order you were directed to place the palm of your right hand on the glass plate in front of you and wait for it to scan and register the contours of your hand.

"No good," the official would say to every single passenger, "wipe your hand on your clothes and try again."

I observed with increasing despondency that there would in every case be several attempts on the part of each passenger before they were told 'OK'. "Now place your left thumb on the glass plate." "No good, try again." Once again, there were several attempts before success. The whole process took around 10 minutes for each passenger and had it not been for another two E-visa entry points opening, the couple of hundred or so travellers behind me would have been there for at least 6 hours.

At last, it was my turn to step forward and I repeated the process I felt the eyes of the great queue of passengers behind, urging me on so that they could have their turn. Eventually, my documents were checked and my palms were successfully scanned and the E-visa operator said 'Welcome to India'. I was very tired and the relief of eventually being allowed in made me quite emotional. I thanked the official in that choked up way.

It was now about 2 am and I made my way to the baggage carousel via a washroom where I took my first drink of tap water in India from my special filter bottle. I wondered if it really did do what it claimed to do. I would find out soon enough.

My bag had been lying waiting for me for several hours. It was like meeting an old friend and I felt whole again. I made my way towards the arrivals entrance via an ATM.

Something worth mentioning about arrival in India is money. You are not meant to bring any Indian currency into the country as it is illegal. You will need to make a beeline for the ATM in the arrivals hall after baggage collection. I withdrew 5000 rupees, or Rs 5000 which is about 50 pounds. The ATM machines like anywhere else are self-explanatory and easy to use.

Tucking my money safely away in the side pocket of my rucksack, I made my way through the automatic doors. The early morning Mumbai air had a balmy warmth about it mixed with not unpleasant but unfamiliar aromas. I thought it was quite noisy for this time of the morning, with scooters, motorbikes, cars and tuk-tuks mingled with familiar airport noises of aircraft and tannoy announcements in all kinds of languages.

There was a line of about 50 taxi drivers and chauffeurs waiting for their passengers. Each was holding a board at chest level with a passenger's name on it. I spotted mine quite quickly and approached the driver who looked pretty tired and un-amused. "Hello, I'm sorry that I'm so late, have you been waiting long?" In pretty good English and a flat expression he said: "Five hours." I couldn't believe that he had been waiting duty bound for all that time without doing something else. However, I thought the best thing was to leave it at that and make sure he had a good tip at the end.

The driver offered to take my bag but I gratefully declined. I felt I wanted to do my bit as a way of saying sorry for keeping him waiting. It occurred to me afterwards that he might have seen my refusal as patronising. Was I saying sorry for me being late or was I trying to demonstrate what a thoroughly good lot us British chaps are?

With my bag slung over my shoulder, we made our way to a poorly lit multi-storey car park. I followed the driver through the dark entrance and up two flights of concrete steps lit by a flickering fluorescent lamp, which attracted various flying insects. The steps were a challenge for my knee, which was once more tender and swollen. The second level was quite empty apart from my jeep like taxi, which was parked at the far end. It occurred to me that earlier the car park may have been full and that this was the nearest to the stairs he could park. Perhaps he really had been waiting 5 hours.

Finally, releasing my rucksack to the driver who hadn't said anything since picking me up at arrivals, he placed it in the boot. Opening the rear door for me to take a seat I said I would prefer to sit in the front with him. He seemed surprised; however I wanted to chat occasionally and didn't want to speak to the back of his head. Before setting off, he walked to what looked like a payment machine and obtained a ticket. It was with some surprise therefore that on our way out of the car park, we were waved down and stopped by a man accompanied by several other men just before the exit. I heard my driver mutter something to himself as he slowly came to a halt and wind down the window.

One of the men peered into the car and looked at me for a few seconds. His eyes were piercing and inquisitive. I didn't think he was a policeman as there was no uniform, but he did have some authority about him. The other men with him stood around our vehicle, eyeing it and muttering between themselves. My imagination came quickly into play and I had images of being pulled from the car and transferred to the boot of another on a long trip to somewhere north. *The British government don't pay ransoms,* I thought. Stupidly, extremely tired, emotional and full of a false sense of security being a British subject and all of that, I smiled at the man and gave him a thumbs up. The man did not smile back. He probably, and quite rightly, might have thought that I was an idiot. He ignored me and turned his attention instead to the driver who had his wallet out. There was no conversation between them. My driver paid him some money and we were allowed to proceed. To this day I have no idea what this was about but I did sense that the whole affair increased my driver's unhappiness and the cloud, which hung over us became darker.

The taxi ride from the airport to my hotel was my first sojourn into India. There was very little conversation other than the usual taxi chat. *He just isn't in the mood,* I thought. We set off along poorly lit streets. Many were narrow and shop-lined while a few were two lane carriageways. As we passed along the narrow streets our headlights briefly illuminated shop doorways. In some, there were people sleeping. Dogs sniffing around the pavements for scraps ignored us as we passed by.

Mumbai is a busy industrious city and even at this hour of the morning there were those who could not afford to sleep and were already at work. We passed women and men carrying large bundles on their heads, which looked heavy and unstable.

Others gathered in large groups waiting for something, perhaps the chance of a job. There was a cow lying in the middle of one of the narrower roads, which my driver skilfully navigated his way around without any indication of irritation. In the UK, we get annoyed if the lights don't turn green quickly enough. *He has done this a thousand times before,* I thought.

It was now around 3 am. The journey through Mumbai to Fort was about 40 minutes but it seemed much shorter. My attention was firmly on the new experience.

We neared the end of our ride. I had a picture of the residency and its surroundings in my mind. A grand entrance in a tree-lined avenue with a smiling doorman in white gloves, cap and uniform opening the taxi door upon my arrival. The reality was slightly different as we emerged from a dim side street into the cul-de-sac, where the residency stood. Here it was slightly better lit. Electrical cables hung precariously above us and down the sides of buildings disappearing into broken looking junction boxes, a few of which appeared to be hanging by one Rawlplug. Pavement paving slabs here and there were broken through their middle. The part nearest the road leaned towards it at a sharp angle making it necessary for any pedestrian to walk into the road to avoid the trip hazard. One or two people slept on the more level sections of the pavements and reminded me of reclining Buddhas.

They slept to the background music of motor scooters and the occasional tuk-tuk. It was now close to 4 am and as busy as an early summers evening in Bournemouth.

The residency entrance was indeed salubrious compared to its surroundings. It looked quite cosmopolitan, with the glow of the modest streetlights reflecting on the four marble steps leading to the entrance door. The door itself was glass with a highly polished brass surround, which reflected not only the street lighting but also the marble steps leading to it.

The driver leapt out of the taxi and took my bag from the boot handing it over to the night concierge who had come out to greet me with a broad smile. His perfectly set white teeth contrasted handsomely with his dark skin. He was a slim, short man who looked to be in his late forties. He had a magnificent handle bar moustache, which was waxed at the ends and stood out either side of his narrow face giving an uncanny resemblance to Salvador Dali. His grey suit, and white shirt and tie, were a perfect match for his highly polished black slip-on shoes which flashed occasionally as they caught and reflected the overhead street lighting as he fussed around the vehicle and me like a mother hen.

I paid the driver Rs 500, which appeared to cheer him up. Apparently Rs 500 is a good tip in Mumbai. For the first time, he smiled as he thanked me and went on his way. I had arranged the taxi through the residency. They paid the driver and I would pay them at the end of my stay. It was about Rs 1000.

The concierge ushered me up the steps allowing me to enter first, pushing open the glass door, which led directly into the air-conditioned lobby, which housed the reception desk. The lobby was pleasantly decorated. There seemed to have been an attempt to reflect a style reminiscent of a Maharaja's palace. There were white walls with golden-stencilled images of tigers and elephants spaced across them at about the height of a dado rail. Two white marbled effect pillars trimmed with gold leaf at their cornices guarded the entrance door just inside. The reception desk and the receptionist were not as grand. It looked as if they had been together since the early 1970s and had resisted any attempts whatsoever to be updated in line with the rest of the lobby. Everything which had changed over the next 30 years seemed to have done so without disturbing either of them. It really was an odd juxtaposition of old and new, but as I was to discover later, this was how it is in Mumbai.

The immaculately dressed concierge, still smiling broadly directed me to the receptionist. After completing the formalities of checking, which included the standard practice of handing over your passport, he presented me with a tray of goodies to take to my room. There were two cans of fizzy orange and different types of biscuits and sweets. Ominously, in a little plastic container were some earplugs. I asked him if it was possible to have a beer, however it was pointed out that it was past 4 am and there was no bar at the hotel anyway. I could have murdered a glass of cold lager before turning in even at this unearthly hour.

It is worth mentioning that if you enjoy alcohol, you should know the rules regarding drinking in India. Mumbai is generally not a problem and there is by all accounts quite a pub culture amongst the wealthier sections of the community. When travelling south to Kerala, the rules get tighter and there are sometimes non-alcohol days declared so it is as well to be aware of that. Of course, as with any prohibition drinking alcohol is simply driven underground and as long as you know where to go you can get a drink. It is just something to bear in mind.

The concierge summoned a porter who took me to a lift and then to my room. The porter opened the door to my room, smiling broadly. He seemed to be proud to do so. Everything was of a very high standard, air-conditioned and extremely clean. The bathroom was very well-designed, ultra-modern and clean.

I had no smaller denomination notes to tip the porter and promised to give him something when I saw him next. He smiled and told me that it was not a problem, although it was a little embarrassing. The job couldn't have paid much and like any other service industry worker, tips are an important part of earnings.

It was 4:30am and I was exhausted. Giving up the unpacking, I switched off the light and clambered into bed. It was so quiet and peaceful. I anticipated waking at around 10 am. I must have fallen asleep very quickly.

It was around 7:30 am. I woke suddenly to a room full of noise and light. From somewhere outside the residency there was, hammering, drilling, shouting and car horns. Bright sun poured through the thin curtains. I got out of bed and pulled them back. Wincing from the bright sunlight I saw India for the first time in daylight.

Just below my window there were extensive building works being done. There was a gigantic hole in the ground with all manner of machinery engineering it. On the other side of the hole was a narrow street with heavy traffic pushing through, horns blaring. I learned later that the hole was a new Mumbai metro being built, and the traffic I saw and which I thought was hellish turned out to be nothing in comparison to what I would witness over the coming 48 hours. Suddenly the significance of the earplugs supplied to me earlier became clear. At best, I had had two and a half hours sleep but it was pointless to try to get more.

I took my time getting ready to explore Mumbai. It's a big place and like India itself, you can't see much of it in a short visit. As with exploring any great city, it's important that you feel comfortably dressed and are well prepared for the long day ahead.

After taking a refreshing shower and getting dressed, I was in gear and ready to go exploring. I chose to wear my chinos again, since they were light and roomy, albeit a little worse for wearing following the events of the past 36 hours. I wore a thin cheese-cloth shirt, which was not tucked in for maximum air circulation. My trainers were the only shoes I had brought with me. I wore my straw trilby style hat. I fancied that I might look like the quintessential Englishman in that hat. Looking back I certainly think I may have looked the part.

Stepping out of the air-conditioned hotel onto the street, the morning heat hit me full on. My recently awakened brain started to make sense of the smells and unfamiliar sights and sounds. Rotten garbage mixed with incense sticks and vehicle fumes made a heady mix. Tuk-tuks raced to and fro carrying their fares. Motorbikes and scooters weaved their noisy way through the busy, crowded streets, pedestrians unmoved by the sound of their horns demanding they step aside.

I hadn't planned anything for this single day in Mumbai. I would have had longer if my flight hadn't been delayed. I thought the first thing I would do was go to the train terminus and find my platform for the next day's epic train journey to Goa. According to some travel books it was recommended that you arrive one hour before departure. This meant being there at 6 am, which would involve a 5 am call. I would have to get to bed reasonably early to be energised for the 12-hour journey on the Mandovi Express.

The walk to the train terminus was only 20 minutes from the residency. I took the residency address with me so that I could be adventurous and get lost if I liked. It would be easy enough to get a cab back. It was a fascinating stroll through the back streets of Fort on the way to the terminus. This was my first experience of daytime India. Either side of the narrow streets there was enterprise. Everyone, it seemed, was busy doing something. Some were bashing metal for one reason or another, while others mended shoes or worked leather. Each entrepreneur was tucked away in a little space, sandwiched between old colonial buildings, which seemed to be crumbling under the weight of time. The paint on the front of them had long since fallen off leaving remnants of different colours from times past with great chunks of plaster or cement missing from their walls. Electricity junction boxes hung precariously from the walls of these buildings and the thick cables going to them swung overhead as I walked along.

There were few shops to speak of in these side streets. They were mostly little booths where you could buy cigarettes, chewing gum, and telephone SIM cards. Amongst it all there were occasional cows, some accompanied by their young slowly making their way through the streets. Local pedestrians took it in their stride and nonchalantly mingled with it all. The cows weren't like the ones back home. They were bony and looked malnourished. I was later to find out that they didn't belong to anyone. They just wandered around free from any human threat and assured of protection if not care.

As I emerged from the shady confines of the narrow side streets, I was met with a sudden and startling tsunami of sound and light. The tempo had changed. I now found myself at a large intersection of several roads flanked by shops, stalls and all manner of street traders. The noise from the traffic jangled the nerves. There were scooters and motorbikes, some, no more than perhaps 250cc carrying two or three children probably on their way to school. Others were laden with bales of paper or huge bags of what looked like laundry or plastic bottles. They weaved their way in and out of the chaos of scores of cars and buses laden with people and goods. Lane control didn't seem to exist. To add to the cacophony of sound was the use of horns. Every vehicle it seemed sounded its horn at every opportunity. Apparently, this was part of the driving technique in India, especially in the larger cities. Sounding your horn appeared to be a way of letting the person in front know that you were behind them and intended to manoeuvre past at some point. This may have been to the left or to the right of them. Another use was to let everyone else know that you were in a hurry and seemed to say: please could the fifty stationary cars in front of you move along or move out of the way. There were plenty of dents and bashes to be seen but no shaking fists or birdies.

To add to the chaos a large lorry laden with steel girders was being marshalled in reverse against the flow of traffic. The marshaller's attempts to stop the approaching traffic to make way for the reversing vehicle were largely ignored, but I feel sure he knew what he was doing and that he would achieve his goal eventually.

The Victoria Terminus, grand and beautiful, appeared just beyond the intersection. It is an impressive building. The terminus was built by Indian labourers under the direction of British architects and engineers and completed in 1888 to commemorate 50 years of rule by Queen Victoria. Despite the buildings association with the British Raj, there is a strong acknowledgement of the beauty of Indian art and architectural design with its elaborate spires perched elegantly on Indian sandstone and limestone towers. The use of marble compliments the structure giving it a sense of strength and stability. Following independence from Britain the station was renamed. Its official name is now the Chhatrapati Shivaji Terminus. It is a UNESCO world heritage site.

Stepping inside the building brought a lump to my throat and took my breath away. The inside was huge and magnificent. The sculptures inside matched that of any great church. There were so many people; some slept alone on the cool marble floor, others together in family groups. I imagined they were waiting for the train, which would take them to a far-off part of India or beyond. Perhaps they had already been on such a journey and were recovering before their connection to complete their journey. It was clear from the many types of clothing styles and headdresses that this was a meeting of many cultures within a culture. Some train journeys from and to Mumbai took in excess of 24 hours and reached as far as the Himalayas.

I remember hearing a story told to me by an usher at Winchester Cathedral a few years ago. They described the English cathedrals at the time of the reformation in the 1500s as cattle sheds and places to trade, sleep and eat. People seemed to have lost their reverence for these places then. It occurred to me that these rail passengers temporarily setting up home in this great building did so with the same indifference to its history and origins as the English in the Middle Ages.

I wandered through the station looking up at the great vaulted ceilings. Without colliding with something or someone, I eventually found my platform. It was clearly marked as platform 17 for the Mandovi express.

It was reassuring to have found the precise starting point for the long journey to Goa in the morning.

5. The Shoe Shine Boy and the Tailor

Having achieved this goal I decided to leave the terminus and explore the southernmost end of Fort. I wanted to see the Gateway of India and the Taj Mahal Hotel, so off I went using the map on my phone and stopping to ask.

Along the way I sampled some delicious street food for my breakfast from the most basic of stalls. I chose Vada Pav, which means Poor Man's Burger. It consists of a mashed potato fritter inside of a bread bun. It is served with fried chillies and sweet, spicy chutney all served up in newspaper arranged in the shape of a bowl. Fingers were the utensils of the day and the hand sanitizer and wipes I had in my bag were useful before and after.

The walk to the India Gate was long and hot. The sights and sounds carried me along and engaged my attention fully, making time irrelevant. Despite having my phone, I avoided using it too much to navigate because it tended to drain the battery and I needed that for photographs. I eventually asked directions to the Gate from an Indian gentleman who I could hear had just finished speaking in English to another European He told me I must make my way first to the Fountain. From there, I would see the signs to the Gate. There was something magical about that. "First you have to find the Fountain." It was like a line from a fairy tale.

Sure enough I found the Fountain, which is known as Flora Fountain. It was erected in 1864 and depicts the Roman goddess Flora. It was situated in gardens, which were well kept, and lush. It felt like a little oasis of peace amongst the noise and heat outside of it. I sat for a while on a cool marble bench and began taking a few photographs on my phone.

A large bearded man approached me. He wore a skull cap, and a long collarless shirt over tightly fitting trousers otherwise known as *churidor* pyjama. "Excuse me, Brother." I felt honoured that a complete stranger in this place would want to speak to me and above all consider me his brother. He wanted to have a selfie with me and I obliged. Before long, a short plump Indian gentleman who by the red *bindi* on his forehead I assumed was Hindu, this time addressed me as 'uncle'. Uncle or auntie is a term of respect for an older man or woman. He asked if he could take a photograph of the Muslim man and I with each of our phones. We gratefully accepted. In return, the Muslim man took a photograph of me with the Hindu gentleman on each of our phones. As this was happening a group of four young Indian men approached calling 'Uncle', and mutual photographic sessions began again. It was quite bazar. I sensed my ego reaching new heights and felt like some sort of celebrity.

Was it the hat and the clothes or something that had spontaneously happened and had got out of hand? Or was it a case of mistaken identity?

As quickly as it had begun the photography session ended and the gathering dispersed. Slightly bemused by this impromptu gathering I walked out of the gardens into the bustle of Fort and made my way through the hot noisy streets again towards the India Gate.

As I made my way past shops, restaurants and various venders selling mobile phones, cheap watches and souvenir fridge magnets, I sensed the saltiness of the sea air as the harbour drew closer.

Mumbai is effectively a group of seven islands surrounded on three sides by the Arabian Sea. Today's Mumbai stands as a monument to human endeavour. It is India's Statue of Liberty, and like the USA, owes its present form to those who throughout history landed on its shores to exploit its position and its resources. Those visitors included the Romans, Greeks, Moguls, Portuguese, and more recently the British Raj. Of those visitors, the Portuguese and the British left the most visible evidence of their occupation through their architecture and churches. The India Gate is an impressive piece of architecture. It is a reminder of past glories and great change over its 100 year history.

The Gate is situated a little way back from the harbour wall. It proudly guards the seafront. Its ornate central arch is 49 feet wide accounting for over half its 85-foot height. Built in 1927 to commemorate the arrival of their Imperial Majesties King George V and Queen Mary in 1911, the Gate would have left no doubt to any visitor arriving at Mumbai by sea, that the British Raj was at home and firmly in charge. That changed with the coming of independence in 1947.

The area around the Gate is a major tourist spot. Photographers vie for the opportunity to take a romantic photograph of you or you and your 'beautiful wife' in front of this iconic structure. Guides offer harbour trips and tours to the ancient Buddhist cave temple of Elephanta Island 7 miles off shore. They earnestly wave their brochures at you insisting that they offer the best prices and that you should come quickly as the boat is going to leave soon.

The Taj Mahal Palace Hotel more affectionately known as the Taj is situated on the opposite side of the road to the Gateway. It is a magnificent building. Built in 1903 with 560 rooms, 44 suites and 9 restaurants. It is considered to be one of the finest hotels in the east since the time of the British Raj.

Both the Gateway and the Taj have been the target of terrorist attacks in the past. In 2003, 54 people were killed in a blast at the Gateway, while in 2008 both the Gateway and Taj were subjected to attacks, which were part of a series of coordinated attacks across India. It is believed that in both cases the attacks were carried out by terrorists from Pakistan seeking revenge for anti-Muslim riots, which were happening across India at the time. The unrest in India during my visit made me feel a little uncomfortable.

There were lots of sightseers taking photographs of the Gate, the Taj and of each other. Again I was asked for a selfie with a gentleman and was approached by a young man who asked me if I had one of my CDs I could give him?

What's going on here? I thought, *who is it that I am inadvertently pretending to be?* At this point my ego was having a feast. I was feeling pretty pleased with myself.

It was lunchtime and I was ready for a beer. I decided to leave the gate and walk through Fort to find somewhere to eat and drink on my way back to the residency. As I stood leaning against a wall in the hot sun studying my route and considering where to get a beer, I was greeted with a "hello Uncle, how are you?" It was a young man probably about 30. He was slim and like many men in Mumbai wore a short-sleeved shirt, jeans and sandals. "I am very well, thank you," I said. We spoke for a short while about nothing much when he said "Can I polish your shoes?" Looking down at my feet I pointed out that they were trainers. He didn't say any more about shoe cleaning but introduced himself as Ishaan. He asked if I was looking for somewhere to eat. I said I was looking for somewhere to have a beer. Ishaan asked me if he could show me a nice place, which was very cheap. I accepted his offer and he led the way walking ahead at some pace.

After a short few minutes, we arrived at a busy side street. It was lined along both sides with small grocery shops. Their colourful vegetables, spices and fruits arranged in wooden boxes took up all of the pavement space, forcing pedestrians to walk in the road. Situated between some of the shops, were workshops. There was hammering and the clunking and grinding of machinery mingled with the smell of welding and hot metal. In addition to the stores and workshops, there were open front kitchens producing breads and aromatic dahls.

Amongst all of this and the heat of the day, I was grateful that we had at last arrived at our watering hole. It was nothing to look at from the front. The walls around the green metal entrance door which was held open by a red plastic beer crate were pitted and the paint had long since fallen off revealing rough plaster and brick. The open doorway was protected against the ingress of flies by a beaded curtain, which somehow caught on the strap of my manbag as we entered the dingy little bar, making my entrance awkward and clumsy. The place was lit with un-shaded light bulbs, which, despite the beaded entrance curtain, attracted flying insects above our heads. We took a seat at what looked like a 1950s melamine table. It wobbled slightly when I rested my arm on it.

The bar was occupied by a handful of men drinking beer and watching cricket on a television, which was mounted on a wall. They would occasionally cast glances in our direction. The bar was dark and after stepping in from the bright daylight outside it took some time for my eyes to adjust. The atmosphere was seedy and edgy.

Ishaan seemed to know some of the men there, exchanging nods with them. I began to feel vulnerable but decided to sit with the discomfort and experience whatever may follow. I recalled some of the old black and white movies of British sailors drinking in smoky dingy dance halls and bars in places like Singapore and old Bombay on runs ashore. The thought momentarily amused me, and for a short few moments the whole situation felt as if I had travelled back in time.

From the shadows of the dimly lit bar, a waiter came to our table. He was overweight for his short stature. His dark, thin moustache and greased back hair reminded me of Agatha Christie's Poirot. Six inches of fat belly hung out from a grubby white vest over the waistline of his ill-fitting jeans. Unsmiling, he appeared to ask Ishaan, presumably in Hindi, what we wanted. Perhaps it was my imagination when I thought there was more being said between them than taking an order. I asked for a beer and Ishaan asked for an orange juice. I asked him if he would like something to eat; I wasn't hungry. He gratefully accepted and told the waiter what he wanted. The man disappeared into the shadows to fetch our order.

While we waited for our order, we chatted about Ishaan's life and I told him a little about my own. His English was good. He told me he lived in the Mumbai slums and came to

Fort daily on the train to clean shoes for a living. He had a wife and two children. He said his dream was to own his own shoe-cleaning box, which would cost him around 2000 rupees. He kept referring to the 2000 rupees, which is about £20. I remember wondering how he was able to clean shoes that day anyway. There was no evidence of shoe cleaning equipment when he first spoke to me in the street and he certainly hadn't brought any with him to this place for safekeeping.

After a short few minutes, the waiter arrived with our drinks. He was carrying our two glasses in his left hand and was holding them on the inside near the rim with his forefinger and thumb on the inside of them. I opted to have the glass being held by the thumb. It occurred to me that a thumb was possibly less active than a forefinger. The glasses and the bottles were placed with a thump on the table and without speaking the waiter left us to our drinks. My beer was a large bottle of Kingfisher lager beer. I filled my glass and drank it quickly to satisfy my thirst. Pouring a second glass I drank more slowly.

While preparing for my trip I had read about things which were to be avoided in India as a single traveller. One of them was accepting drinks, which had not been prepared in front of you. Apparently, there have been instances where tourists on their own have been drugged and robbed; some reports were of kidnapping and rape. Having drunk the best part of my large bottle of lager, it occurred to me that the bottle had had its top removed prior to it coming to the table. As the thought entered my mind, I noticed a feeling of mild numbness developing in my face and I could feel my attention wandering. I quickly came to the conclusion that my drink had been spiked and that I may lose consciousness quite soon. I had to get out of the bar to the relative safety of the street. Ishaan must have seen the look of anxiety on my face as I became restless and inattentive.

Standing unsteadily, I dropped 500 rupees on the table to cover the order and told Ishaan that he could keep the change. The room now felt as if it was swaying slightly. Ishaan looked mystified and was no doubt disappointed that his potential shoebox was leaving so abruptly.

Without saying goodbye I made my way to the exit touching tables on my way out for security in case I should stumble. The waiter who had served us seemed to be monitoring my departure. Perhaps it was him that had spiked my drink and was waiting for me to crumble into a heap before bundling me into a back room for processing.

Getting out into the open was a relief. The daylight greeted me like an atomic flash and I recoiled from its intensity instinctively pulling my hand up to shield my eyes. I had to get away from that place. I had thoughts of being stalked just as a lion would stalk an injured animal until it finally succumbs and lays down in surrender before being dragged back to the lair.

The mind is a powerful thing. I finally calmed down and as I walked somewhat shaken along the Mumbai streets, the drama, which had previously unfolded, lost its power and once again I felt reasonably safe, albeit still fuzzy headed.

The sensation of being drugged was now wearing off and I decided to get something to eat and drink in a modern high street restaurant.

The restaurant I found was indeed modern. There were smartly turned out waiters and the tables were dressed with tablecloths and napkins. Taking a seat by a window so that I could people watch, I ordered a Kingfisher and some spicy fried okra. As I drank the beer, I noticed that feeling of warm sleepiness coming back again. This time, however, the bottle had been opened and poured in front of me by a waiter. The half full bottle was left on the table for the waiter to pour when my glass needed refilling. I looked carefully at the bottle as you may gaze at a ketchup or mayo bottle as you eat your meal. I noticed that the Kingfisher label was a different colour to the ones in the UK. It was a darker shade of red and looking more closely I read Kingfisher extra 8% ABV. It dawned on me that I hadn't previously been drugged at all. That first drink of the day was almost twice the strength of anything I normally drink at home. I reflected on the events of the past hour and smiled at my overactive mind.

Having had a delightful lunch, it was time to wander back to my hotel. In high spirits, I found myself entering a busy marketplace. It was colourful and noisy with traders selling their wares either side of a narrow pavement, which created a passageway that extended for the whole length of the road upon which it stood. Incense, spices and leather goods provided a heady mix of fragrances. There were mobile phone stalls, clothes and the usual tourist gift stalls selling fridge magnets and badges with big red hearts proclaiming a love for Mumbai. Every so often, someone would approach me and enthusiastically invite me to come to their shop, "just for a look, no obligation to buy." They were tailors and their mission was to get a visitor like me to follow them out of the market to a shop in a side street to have a suit or shirts, tailor made in a matter of hours. As I walked along, I batted them off like flies with a polite shake of the head and a "no thank you, not today." But they are persistent. If you say, "not today" they say "when then?"

I eventually succumbed after one of these tailors managed to strike up a conversation with me. He skilfully manipulated my alcohol fuelled ego by paying compliments about my hat of all things. In no time, this ego driven idiot followed the tailor to his side street shop. I removed my trainers and entered.

The shop was piled high with bales of cloth of all sorts of colours, patterns and textures. "There is no obligation sir, all I ask is for you to take some chai with me or perhaps a beer and let me show you some fine examples of suits and shirts which can be made for you within 12 hours."

I declined the offer of a beer for fear of losing any self-control I may still have. Out of politeness I accepted the offer of chai. He clicked his fingers and sent his assistant scurrying outside of the shop presumably to find a chai seller.

Moments later the assistant returned with the delicious sweet tea. The tailor and I talked for a while about his business and the service he offered. I finished my tea and stood to leave, thanking him for his hospitality and interesting insights into his business. As I did, two of his assistants armed with tape measures approached me. As I shuffled towards the door trying to put my trainers back on, one was measuring my neck the other was measuring my inside leg. It must have looked like a sort of rugby tackle.

Bending forward to ease my left trainer on with one finger down the back of my heal, a bail of cloth was pushed under my nose. "We only use the very best available cloth in India sir." "One pair of trousers only sir, we will have them ready for you to wear today."

Gradually and very skilfully they wore me down. I agreed to have two pairs of trousers and two shirts made. I would collect them when I returned to Mumbai in a week. "Thank you for your order sir," he said. "How about a nice suit?"

"No, thank you," I said.

"I definitely do not need a suit," I said.

"But you do," he said. "And when you return from your travels, I will definitely sell you one," he said smiling broadly, punching the air with his fist. I paid for my order, smiled and left feeling well and truly defeated. It occurred to me that the tailor had punched the air not so much because of the money but because of the victory of the sale.

A tuk-tuk ride in Mumbai is interesting. I took one from the marketplace to the residency. It really is a good way to get in and out of the hellishly busy traffic. Fearlessly and fully in the moment, the driver took me weaving and swaying through the horn blowing congested traffic with the ease of a hot knife going through butter. Arriving back at my hotel, I thanked my driver and gave him a Rs 200 tip.

It was going to be a big day tomorrow and I had a very early start. I was extremely tired and I didn't intend being late to bed. By the time, I had showered and organised myself, it was around 6:30 pm and getting dark. Still tired yet buzzing from my day out, I made my way downstairs to reception to ask about any recommendations for eating out. Upon entering the foyer, I was greeted by a very smartly dressed concierge. He was about forty, slim and around 5'10". His cream high-neck tunic, embroidered with gold complimented his fine dark features. He was without doubt a handsome man. Beneath his long tunic he wore matching cream trousers and sandals.

He bade me a good evening and with a charming smile, asked if there was anything he could do to help this evening. I asked him if there was a nice restaurant with a bar nearby. He told me there was and that he would show me. "But first, sir," he said, "may I show you something and ask your opinion?"

I was surprised that this stranger, in a foreign land, would want my opinion about anything. Intrigued, I agreed, and followed him out of the air-conditioned hotel into the busy evening street. It was now around 7 pm and the evening was only a little cooler than the afternoon. Emerging from the relatively quiet hotel into the Mumbai evening woke every sense again. The street was filled with the noise of scooters whining their way through the narrow streets. Unseen tuk-tuk engines as familiar to me by then as an out of sight Spitfire added to the wall of sound. As with many countries with a warm climate outside in the evening air, music could be heard, announcing the time for leisure. The smell of evening meals came from unseen places and mingled with vehicle fumes, incense and garbage.

We walked just a few short yards from the hotel, before turning a corner. We had arrived at a narrow ally-way. There, proudly standing next to an old paint-flecked wall supported on its stand, which rested precariously on an uneven pavement, was the object he wished me to give my opinion about. It was a Honda 250cc motorcycle, which was gleaming and new. A flickering neon sign sporadically illuminated the ally-way and reflected in the highly polished black paintwork of the petrol tank, and chrome work making the bike flash like a Christmas decoration. "Do you like it, sir?" He said beaming widely. I did, and showed my admiration for his new purchase, stroking it lightly and noting the dials and immaculate engine with 'very nice' repeated sincerely several times. He was obviously very proud of it and I felt privileged that he had asked me, a complete stranger, to see his pride and joy. I seemed to make connections very quickly with Indian people. Did they see gullibility or was I in some way approachable? Perhaps most westerners have the same experience.

"Wow, very nice," I said, noting the Honda badge. I mentioned that I once had a Honda. It seemed that at that moment my statement had somehow forged a connection between us. "Come," he said, enthusiastically, "let's go for a ride, I will take you to the restaurant, they are friends of mine and they will look after you."

A surge of excitement took me by surprise. Remembering the advice given in the guidebooks about riding on motorbikes in Mumbai or anywhere else in India as being dangerous and an absolute no, I climbed onto the bike like a naughty defiant child, hooking my sore and swollen knee awkwardly over the seat. No helmet and gripping the back bar tightly we charged noisily through the side streets. The horn constantly blew as we weaved our way, lurching to a stop occasionally to give way to a cow or vehicle appearing from seemingly nowhere. I hadn't felt as alive for a long time.

After an exhilarating 10 minutes, we pulled up outside a warmly lit restaurant, which sat confidently among the chaos of yet another side street. My heart was racing as we came to a halt. Shakily, I let go of the back bar unfolding my stiff sweaty fingers one at a time. An Indian man, perhaps in his fifties, with an air of authority came out of the restaurant to greet us as we arrived. He greeted the concierge, and smiling broadly, welcomed me to his 'most excellent restaurant'.

Before I could thank my lift, he had turned his bike around and sped off into the night. "Come sir, I will look after you," the manager said. We waited for a cow to walk by and entered the restaurant, me awkwardly, due to a struggle with the metal-chained fly screen guarding the entrance. Not for the first time today, had I become entangled with the strap attachments on my manbag.

The restaurant was nice enough. There were about 30 tables, most with four chairs. Each table had been set out neatly with a crisp looking white tablecloth, napkins, knives and forks and a finger bowl. I was shown to a table for two by the manager. The place was nicely decorated and had murals painted on all walls depicting cartoon type characters enjoying meals and catching fish. The evening was young and already the place was quite busy. Waiters scurried in and out of swinging saloon type doors delivering food, clearing tables and setting up new ones for the next customers.

In many places in India, people use their right hand to eat rather than use a knife and fork so I looked around to see what other customers were doing. I came to the conclusion that it depended upon what it was you were eating. If you could easily fold a piece of flat bread in your right hand and scoop up some *dal* with it before popping it into your mouth that was the thing to do. If you had a piece of meat or fish beyond bite size, you would need to use a knife and fork to cut it presumably. Why the right hand? Traditionally the left is used for washing your bottom after you have been to the toilet instead of using paper. The left hand, therefore, is considered to be unclean. Washing your bottom seems much nicer than toilet paper if you don't mind getting stuck in. The right or clean hand is used in preference to the left for many other daily activities including handling money. Being left handed myself sometimes made things awkward.

The menu was extensive but basic and included many dishes available in the UK. I felt a little disappointed that I was unable to try something more unusual. I opted for a *dal* and bread with a side dish of onions and okra. It was OK.

Feeling quite full and unable to drink any more beer, I paid my bill, which came to less than £10 with drinks. The manager had been very attentive throughout my stay. He made sure I never picked my bottle of beer up to pour it. He was there to do that at just the right point every time. I left promising to visit again upon my return to Mumbai. This seemed to please the manager greatly as he shook my hand rigorously and gave me a sweet to suck on my way back to the residency.

I don't know how I found my way back. I suppose I headed in a general direction, picking out landmarks along the way. I did see a cow I recognised, however, it occurred to me that it might have travelled a bit since three hours ago.

I had a big day ahead of me the next morning. When I eventually got back, I asked for a 5 am wake-up call. It was now 11 pm and to date I had had very little sleep since leaving Heathrow two days ago. I wasted no time in going to bed leaving bag packing for the long journey ahead until the morning.

6. The Mandovi Express

I slept soundly. As I dropped off, the events of the past 48 hours merged with the sleepy fantasies of what may follow. The telephone next to my right ear rang promptly at 5 am.

Sleepily aware that this was an important moment, I moved my legs to the edge of the bed and like a hypnotists audience participant, I sat, paused, and then moved zombie like to the bathroom.

A shower woke me up. I dressed, packed my rucksack and went down to reception to settle my bill before making my way out into the relatively cool early morning air. It was still dark and the quietest I had known Mumbai to be since my arrival. There was still warmth in the air but it felt damp and humid.

There was hardly any traffic as I made my way through the narrow streets retracing my steps from the previous day. There was hardly anyone around, apart from the occasional person sleeping in a doorway. Every now and then I had to walk around a cow or two, dozing on the narrow pavements. It was after all very early by anyone's standards.

My haversack felt heavier this morning and my knee was sore from all of the walking I had done the day before. The railway terminus was only 20 minutes' walk.

The crossroads, which before were a death-defying leap of faith, were no busier now than a Sunday morning at Piccadilly Circus. I was able to cross with confidence.

I was approaching the terminus by the back entrance this time. As I got nearer, I could see a line of at least thirty people sleeping on the pavement leading to the entrance. They were women and they all slept with their feet facing towards the road upon which I was now walking. There was nothing between them apart from their belongings, which looked like some bowls, and plates. They slept side by side in a long row like sardines in a tin. I thought they might be terminus workers. After all, for what little they may have been paid I don't suppose they could possibly afford rented accommodation. I wondered how they got on in the rainy season. There was no shelter out there on the street.

Walking past them I shrugged my shoulders and muttered something like, "Ah well, that's India." This wasn't the last time I was to miss an opportunity to express a more compassionate view.

Confident due to my reconnaissance the previous day, I entered the terminus and made my way to my platform on the far side of the station. Its remoteness set it apart from the rest of the station, which reminded me of Harry Potter and Platform 9 ¾.

The station was now beginning to get busy, one big train arriving with its passengers from some far-flung place after an all-night journey across India woke things up a bit. Its great diesel engine roared as it pulled up to the empty platform spilling scores of weary passengers out onto it.

Other trains began to wake up and seemed to yawn, exercising their great diesel driven lungs, which bellowed fumes out into the early morning air.

On my way through to my platform, I noticed passengers who had spent the night sleeping on platforms and in the main terminus were now beginning to exercise their own lungs, stretching and rubbing their eyes. This ritual had been played out every morning for the past 132 years I thought.

I sat on a concrete plinth, which accommodated one of the many huge iron pillars supporting the Victorian iron and glass roof above me, and waited for the Mandovi express. It was good to get the heavy haversack off of my shoulders.

The platform was beginning to fill with passengers now and I wondered which one of them I might be sharing the next 12 hours with. While waiting, I struck up a conversation with the only other European I had seen that morning. He was French and he was getting the same train as me. He would be getting off well before me to continue his journey across central Maharastra. His shoulder length, fair dreadlocks went well with his thin pale-skinned bearded face. He wore baggy dark coloured trousers, which gathered at the ankles and a cream collarless cheesecloth shirt, which was overhung by two long of strings wooden beads. He told me he had been in India for about three months and was used to travelling rough. He had slept on the cool marble station floor that night. You can live and travel in India for very little money if you wish. No one bats an eyelid if you sleep in a railway station, and food is cheaper than chips if you care to live on street food.

As we chatted, a young lad wheeling a battered stainless-steel urn on a trolley approached us shouting, "chai, chai." I was keen to buy some since I hadn't had breakfast and was still a little hung-over and no doubt dehydrated from the previous day. I offered to buy one for the Frenchman, which he gratefully accepted. The sweet aromatic tea cut through my thirst and its sugar rush was comforting.

With 20 minutes before its due departure to Goa, the Mandovi express arrived slowly at the platform, engine slowing down to a noisy idle. The great diesel seemed bigger than the ones in the UK. Its yellow and green livery and square, flat, tough features made it look more like the engineering servicing diesels you see parked up in the sidings of our railway stations in the UK. Its carriages were of different colours. Two or three in a row were red then there were four blue ones together. I speculated that the colours corresponded to different classes of travel. The carriages had manually operated doors and it took me back to the sixties to hear the slamming of doors.

I said goodbye to the Frenchman and we went in different directions to find our carriages. There was plenty of time to board. It was just as well, since I struggled to find the right carriage and then the right compartment and seat. I managed eventually with the help of a very kind gentleman man who knew the routine and what my ticket meant.

He could probably see I was confused. To be fair, if I had read the ticket information carefully, I would have managed.

My compartment was a second-class sleeper, which was curtained off from the central passageway that ran the length of the carriage. The compartment consisted of two, two beaded bunk beds facing each other with enough floor space between them for anyone sitting on the bottom bunks to face each other without knee contact. I had booked the lower bunk window side. It was very clean in the compartment and I couldn't help compare it to the state of the South West Train service form Waterloo to Portsmouth. There were no suspicious sticky puddles on the floor or discarded newspapers or sandwich packets left by the previous occupants.

Each bunk had been supplied with bedding. There were two crisp white sheets, two pillows with freshly laundered cases and two woollen blankets. The seat was a plastic covered mattress, which was firm and felt clean to sit on. It was quite cool due to the air-conditioning. I remember the French hippy laughing when I told him I had an air-conditioned carriage. "Man, you'll freeze your nuts off," he had said. Well, it wasn't quite that bad.

Occupying the bunk opposite me was an elderly Indian lady. She was wearing a red *sari* trimmed with gold thread. She acknowledged me with a flourish of her elaborately patterned henna-stained hand as I entered the compartment. She was very thin with sparrow like features. Several gold bangles decorated the wrinkled friable brown skin, which covered her skinny arms and wrists. Despite her advanced age, she sported several gold piercings in her ears and nose, which I thought made her look proud and dignified. She rightly deserved the respectful title 'aunty' used in India for older ladies.

I said hello and smiled as I self-consciously arranged my things before settling into what I hoped was my seat. The lady seemed to be observing my nest making; smiling slightly, I thought. She spoke no English as far as I could tell; however, she had a look of wisdom about her which put me on my guard against doing anything which may make me look stupid.

So far, it was just me and Aunty sitting in silence in the compartment. As we both had a window seat on the bottom bunk, we sat facing each other. I sensed Auntie staring at me as I saw both of our reflections in the window as I gazed out of it. It was slightly uncomfortable and I avoided making direct eye contact with her until at exactly five minutes past seven the engine roared into action and began to trundle slowly along the track out of the station to begin its long journey.

Looking once more at Auntie with a smile, acknowledging we were at last on our way, she continued to look at me without batting an eyelid or smiling back. I returned to gaze out of the window once again.

It was exciting to begin the journey, albeit a very long one. I remember feeling proud that I had managed to arrange things myself and without any guidance from a travel agent. There were times over the previous twelve months, however, when the smallest of reasons may have been the excuse I needed to back out of the idea of going to India. I think it was the thought of being alone which made me feel uncomfortable.

The train slowly made its way past shabby buildings and makeshift shelters made of odd bits of wood, corrugated iron and plastic sheeting. These were the homes of railway folk. Generation after generation they lived, loved and died in these places. In his book *From Sea to Sea,* published in 1900, Rudyard Kipling wrote a chapter entitled 'Among the Railway Folk'. He tells us that "the railway folk in India have their own language and life which an outsider cannot hope to understand." Here they were, living beside the very tracks laid by their ancestors. Their culture and way of life unlike any other, long established, no doubt with their own folklore and railway deities. A reincarnated Rudyard travelling with me in that carriage would give them a nod and a smile.

The first stop came only 10 minutes after pulling away from the CST. The station was Dadar, a busy shopping area of Mumbai. We stopped for several minutes for more passengers to board. I remember wondering who may join Aunty and I but on this occasion it was no one.

As we set off again, Mumbai gave way to alternating scenes of buildings, scrubland and fields. I couldn't help thinking how similar it was to pulling out of Waterloo and travelling west past factories and houses in various states of disrepair before being absorbed into the English countryside.

After a short while, and to some relief on my part, Aunty decided to sleep. She arranged her bedding starting with a blanket on the plastic mattress first, then a sheet, another blanket, one pillow under her head, and the other under her legs. She pulled both the sheet and the blanket over her head and disappeared under them. I guessed she had done this many times before and would sleep until reaching her destination wherever that may be.

The next stop came after a further 20 minutes. The station was called Thane. In 1853, it was the first passenger rail terminal in Asia. Thane is a city and the 15th most populated in India.

As we sat waiting to depart there was a distant shout from onboard the train. The shout became louder as a chai seller approached our compartment. Chai is lovely and seems to come in all sorts of different flavours. "Chai?" he said as he poked his head through the curtains of the compartment. I nodded and handed him 20 rupees, which is about 20 pence. He poured the chai into a small paper cup and handed it to me piping hot from an urn he had on a small trolley. At that, a hand appeared from under Aunty's blanket opposite and waved around in the air. Aunty never even emerged from under her blanket but the signal she gave was unmistakeable and both the chai seller and I knew exactly what it meant. He poured her chai and I gave him 20 rupees. I placed the paper cup on the little table we both shared next to the window and gently said, "Chai, Aunty." "OK, thank you, leave it on the table," she said in perfect English.

As the train pulled away from Thane a ticket inspector appeared at the entrance to the compartment. He was a fairly tall chubby man with greying neatly cut short hair and a contrasting thin black moustache. He was wearing a dark brown suit and white shirt. A blue tie, which didn't match his suit was tied in a very small knot around his barely discernible neck. I couldn't help noticing that he appeared to have enormous feet, which were accommodated in brown sandals.

Referring to a printed list of what I thought must be passenger names he raised his head towards me and without speaking pointed to the paper ticket I was holding. This was my next challenge. Was I on the right train or even in the right carriage in the right seat? This was the first time anyone had checked my ticket; the one I had printed off at home. The one that I had booked through an agent in Thailand.

The ticket inspector never bothered Aunty who by now had come out of hibernation momentarily, lifting the chai from the little table and disappearing with it under her bedding. I rose from my seat and gave the inspector my ticket. He looked at it and shook his head with an expressionless face. He handed it back to me and moved on to the next carriage. I was left uncertain about my entitlement to be on the train. Perhaps the next stop would be my last. I later learned that the shaking of the head is not disapproval. It is a non-verbal meaning OK.

The next visitor to the carriage about an hour later was a short thin middle-aged man wearing black trainers and dressed in white trousers and vest wearing a white catering hat. He gave me a menu to look at. The only thing I could recognise was vegetarian breakfast, so I went for that, ticking the box with the pencil he loaned me. I pointed at Aunty who was still under her bedding and he shook his head again presumably indicating that all was well and he knew what she wanted.

Within a short few minutes breakfast appeared; from where I do not know. It was a waxed paper container with a lid crimped in place just like our takeaway containers at home. Along with that came what turned out to be *chapatti* bread, which was hot and wrapped in tin foil. I opened the container and saw that breakfast was a vegetable *masala* curry sauce. No vegetables could be found, just sauce. There was loads of it and I got tucked in, greedily scooping it up with my bread. Despite being curry for breakfast, I was really hungry and enjoyed every drop. By the time I had finished, it was pretty messy. As a novel experience, I ate with my fingers as the Indians do. It was the first time I had done so but since Aunty was still under her covers and there was no one else in the carriage I thought I would give it a go. It was all over my hands. My chino trousers were now stained with the yellow sauce and I could only imagine what my face looked like.

There were some tissues provided with the meal but they were not enough. I had to find the toilets and have a clean-up. Not for a moment did I have any concerns about my belongings; however, I did take my passport and visa with me as a precaution. The short walk along the passageway to the toilets took me past other compartments. Some were fully occupied and with their curtains pulled back I couldn't resist peering in at the occupants now eating their breakfasts. Looking up at me as I passed by, I must have looked a sight to them.

I found the unisex toilet, which was very basic but clean. Two footplates and a hole in the floor, with a hand operated hose for washing your bottom and sluicing around the hole and footplates hung securely on the wall beside me as I took a pee. Tissues were provided for drying off and the sink provided hot and cold water for washing. A soap dispenser with pleasant smelling soap was provided.

My observation of the toilet facility in this second-class carriage toilet is that it was far cleaner than most toilets on cross country trains in the UK. I wondered what it would be like in 12 hours' time.

I had taken my Life Straw bottle with me to fill with water from wherever I may find some. Such was my confidence in the cleanliness of everything and the effectiveness of my life-straw, that I filled my water bottle from the tap in the toilet. I never contracted a stomach infection throughout my visit to India. I believe I owed this to good hand hygiene, my Life Straw filtration system, drinking bottled beer and chai and not eating salads. Unbeknown to me at the time, hand hygiene would be a good habit to get into and that the whole world would be joining me soon enough.

When I had returned to my compartment, Aunty had surfaced and was eating her breakfast, which was cheese sandwiches. She had probably arranged for her meals in advance. She soon finished eating and bought another cup of chai from the boy who had remained on the train and had returned to our compartment. I ordered one too and offered to pay for hers again but she declined in Hindi with a "nay." She then disappeared under her bedding again.

The journey so far had been interesting and the time had passed quickly. The train stopping every 30 minutes or so to let passengers, chai seller's, and food vendors to get on and off.

We were now about three hours out of Mumbai and had just stopped at a small town called Mangaon. Just as the train began to pull away, two passengers appeared at the curtain of the compartment. They were both quite large and in their early 60s by the look of them. The gentleman had an outdated look and reminded me of a character in a 1970s Starsky and Hutch film. His grey suit trousers had a slight flare and his matching jacket would not have done up over his very large protruding belly which must have got in the way of most daily activities. His matching grey shirt was open necked and fanned back over the lapels of his jacket.

He was about five foot eight and his frame seemed to struggle to support him as he stood panting and wiping perspiration from his chubby round face after the effort of getting on to the train and walking the few feet from the carriage entrance door to the compartment. The lady, I guessed, was his wife. She wore a dark blue *sari* trimmed with gold.

I thought she had a slightly European look about her. She was a similar height to her husband. Her black hair was tied neatly back in a bun and her paler skin was complimented with red lipstick, red *bindi*, heavy black eye makeup and gold dangling earrings with a small piercing in her nose of a gold stud with a red stone inset. They both huffed and puffed as they entered the carriage. The lady carried the bags as her husband standing behind her guided her large frame into the compartment. Leaving the bags on the floor just by the curtained entrance she sat down with a bump at Aunty's feet. Aunty stirred and began to push back the bedding and sit up.

Aunty and I had the two bottom bunks so I guessed they had the top ones. The only way for them to access their bunks was via a thin metal ladder at the end by the curtained entrance. There was no way that either of them would have managed it. I smiled at them and moved up to make room and invite the man to take a seat on the end of my bunk. I guessed this would be the conventional thing to do unless one of you wanted to lie down to sleep.

No sooner had they settled than out came the food. It was now about 11 am and I hadn't long had my curry breakfast from which I was stuffed. The lady took a large plastic bag from one of two very full plastic shopping bags, which, without any assistance from her travelling companion, she had just hauled into the compartment along with a large bulging suitcase. From it, she scooped up a pile of what looked like small crumbly savoury biscuits in her cupped hands and passed them to her husband. Aunty had now become quite alert and sat chatting to them in Hindi. Before long, she was offered a handful of the biscuits.

I pretended not to see so that I wouldn't get drawn in and offered some of their food. They were clearly caring and sharing people. I stared intently out of the train window as we trundled along determined not to make eye contact with any of them. I just wasn't hungry after my breakfast and besides, taking food from the naked hands of a complete stranger made me feel somewhat uncomfortable. There was no avoiding it though. A prod in the shoulder from my bunk companion made me turn from the window to be greeted with my very own handful of savoury biscuits. "Here, try," the gentleman said smiling at me with pride. "My wife made these this morning for the journey," I smiled back and hesitantly said, "thank you." Aunty looked at me and smiled in a satisfied way knowing I was feeling uncomfortable. I was sure she was having fun with me.

Taking one very small biscuit from the top of the pile he was offering me, hoping to avoid anything which had made contact with his bare palms, I popped it in my mouth smiling and making noises of approval. "No, please, these are yours," he said. I experienced a feeling of dread. I didn't want to offend by refusing but at the same time I was sure that eating these would be my undoing.

I decided in that moment of discomfort that this was something I had to do in the name of adventure and appreciation of their kindness. Holding out my accepting cupped hands he tipped the biscuits into them and to my horror brushed his own together vigorously over mine ensuring I received every last crumb.

My awkward attempts to eat from my hands as a pig would from a trough were relieved by the suggestion of the lady to place the pile on a serviette, which she offered me. I transferred the pile of savouries to the paper trying to turn the pile over as it fell in order to avoid the hand brushings. I cautiously started to eat, being careful to show my appreciation to them both with sounds of enjoyment and mouth shut smiles. To be fair, the biscuits were very nice.

They were about an inch square, crunchy, and had a fresh cumin sort of flavour with a hint of chilli.

Food is always an occasion but more so, I feel, when strangers are gathered together and share it. There was a lot of chatter in Hindi between them and Aunty as we munched noisily through the biscuits. The couple spoke enough English to be friendly towards me but Aunty stuck to Hindi and remained a mystery.

I sat listening, gazing at the Indian countryside as it moved past my window with the speed of a suburban train in England. Picking my way through the remaining biscuits I thought about when the best time would be to fold the serviette over to avoid those last hand rub crumbs and throw it in a bin. The opportunity came when a cleaner appeared at the curtains and proceeded to sweep the floor and take away our rubbish.

Next on the menu was fruit. Out came another bag and chopped fruit was passed around the compartment. Now there is plenty of advice in the travel brochures and books about avoiding an upset stomach in India. Eating peeled fruit is one of those foods to avoid unless you have prepared it yourself. Peeled, it could have been washed in ordinary tap water and since you would avoid drinking it neither should you eat it. This time I had to be firm and refused with gratitude for the kind offer. "Oh my God," the lady said as I raised my hand and said, "Oh no, thank you." "Have you got stomach problems?" she said. Thinking quickly so that I didn't insult her I said that I couldn't eat another thing after her delicious biscuits and that I was quite full. She did that head shake thing and said "OK." I reckoned Aunty understood the situation. She sat on the edge of her bed opposite me with a wry knowing smile on her face again making direct eye contact with me. I smiled back and returned to looking out of the window. She was having fun with my discomfort. Schadenfreude!

Before long, it was lunch. The man in white kitchen gear came around again to take our orders but this time I declined. I was so full and anyway it looked from the menu, which was in English as well as Hindi, that it was pretty much the same as breakfast. My companions ordered theirs. I wondered at the amount of food these people consumed.

They never seemed to stop. I noticed that Aunty, although only very skinny, had a huge stomach bulging out from under her *sari* and speculated that she was either full of food or that something wasn't quite right. The food arrived and everyone ate heartily. The conversation flowed like they had known one another for years.

Throughout the journey I couldn't help detecting a bit of a whiff every now and then. Earlier it was just a whiff but now it was accompanied by a definite fart, which had grown louder, and prouder as the man began to lift his cheek from my bunk bed and push one out every five minutes or so followed by an ahh! I know that this can occur after a meal, however, it is usually dealt with discretely and out of earshot. I imagined that this gentleman had been advised by his ayurvedic practitioner to let go freely and without embarrassment. His wife never showed any sign of disapproval and neither did Aunty. It crossed my mind that this may be a cultural thing and that soon they may all join in. The brass band accompanying Yellow Submarine by the Beatles came to mind. It was time to stretch the legs and get out of there for a while hoping that the air may have cleared upon my return.

Upon my return, life in carriage 4342 had settled down. I could see a postprandial nap descending upon them. Aunty had already disappeared under her blankets again and the lady was standing looking at the top bunk. She moved towards the narrow metal ladder, which she would need to climb if she was to get to her bunk.

She put one foot on the first rung and her husband stood behind her pushing her large bottom as she tried to make it to the second rung. What a struggle it was! Huffing and puffing and 'nay' 'nay' from the lady. I stood up and moved towards them. "Does your wife want to sleep?" I asked the man.

"Yes, she gets very tired. She has recently had heart surgery."

Oh my God, I thought. "Please," I said motioning towards my bunk. "Please let her have mine, I will not be using it or the bedding to sleep on this journey." The couple gratefully accepted my offer. The lady made the bed up and got between the sheets and blankets. Laying her head on the pillows she quickly drifted off to sleep, snoring loudly. I sat on the end of my bunk next to her feet while the man did the same on Aunty's. "Thank you," he said as we both sat knee to knee, him looking intently into my eyes, me trying to avoid eye contact reading Rudyard Kipling's *From Sea to Sea.*

I like Kipling's work, Despite accusations of unacceptable right wing views by today's standards, his writing does show a sensitively and understanding of the culture and the plight of the Indian people under British rule, his poem, *Gunga Din* being an example.

The journey continued and the ladies slept station after station. It was now around 4 pm and we were due to arrive at a station called Kankavali. I gathered this was where my two travelling companions would be taking leave of me as the gentleman gave his wife a gentle wake up prod and he started gathering their bags together.

As we pulled into the station, they both thanked me for the use of my bed and waddled off down the passageway to the exit. Aunty remained asleep under her bedding.

Shortly after the couple left and the train was on its way once more, Aunty stirred and began to prepare herself for what looked like her departure. Sure enough, as we approached Sindhudurg, not far from the Goan border, she began to make her way out of the carriage. The train came to a halt and I offered to carry her bag, which she accepted with the usual head movement meaning OK. Turning to me as I helped her off with her bag she smiled and in perfect English, said, "I hope you enjoy your visit to India, don't forget to wash your hands frequently." I felt duped.

The chatter, laughter and faint sound of Indian popular music had now subsided from the accompanying compartments which were now only occupied by one or two travellers. Alone in my compartment, I reflected with a smile on the events of the day. There was a realisation that this journey would remain in my memory for a very long time.

It was now only three hours until Madgoan and the end of my Mandovi Express experience. I felt able to stand and stretch my legs a bit now that I had the compartment to myself. I wandered to and fro between compartment and passageway exercising my knee, which had become stiff after all of the sitting. Gazing out at the passing countryside I guessed we must be in the process of crossing into Goa from Maharashtra. The train passed over several bridges, which spanned some very impressive rivers and waterways suggesting an interstate border.

The passing scenery was becoming very picturesque. Isolated temples appeared occasionally at the edge of paddy fields and the sun – which was getting low now – reflected its deepening orange on their whitewashed walls and pink domes. My imagination began to paint pictures about what lay ahead.

In the following few hours, station after station seemed to come in quick succession. With less than an hour to go before the end of my journey, there was no one else to be seen in my carriage apart from the cleaner who, as he had done throughout the entire journey, swept and collected any rubbish that had been left, keeping the compartments spotless. His colleague was doing his rounds also, collecting bedding from each compartment for washing before the return journey in the morning.

It was now around 7 pm, almost 12 hours since leaving Mumbai and the last of the sun had gone. Last checks around the compartment to make sure nothing had been left made me ready for my arrival. I took myself, and my haversack to the passageway and stood waiting for my destination. Soon enough, dimly lit signs by the side of the track saying Madgoan began to appear as the train slowly trundled to a halt. I had arrived in Goa.

7. Goa and the French Connection

Stepping off of the train onto the platform, the warm early evening air felt cleaner than Mumbai's; apart from the familiar railway engine smells of hot wheels, grease and diesel. With my rucksack slung over one shoulder, I felt excited and mildly relieved that this part of my adventure had now been completed and the next was to unfold.

The platform was a busy, noisy place. The number of passengers emerging from the other carriages of my train surprised me. The station PA system never stopped. Arrivals and departures were made in English and every Hindi dialect – of which there are many – by a female with a very shrill voice.

I followed the other passengers up a flight of well-worn metal stairs and over an insanely busy footbridge leading to the exit. With no passenger lane control, it was chaotic and a real struggle to get to the exit. Large numbers of passengers were coming from the opposite direction. I remember thinking how useful it was to agree to walk on the right regardless of your direction of travel on the London underground.

The noise and chaos continued as I emerged from the footbridge at the exit. There were scores of men standing around, chatting, smoking, and laughing to the background din of tuk-tuks, motorbikes, scooters and horns. They were all taxis; you could hire any one of the various modes of transport to get you to your destination. My host in Agonda had arranged for a taxi to meet me and take me on the forty-minute journey. I was to meet the driver at the main entrance to the station at 7.30 pm. With half an hour to spare, I had time for a beer if I could find one.

"Sir, Sir, Uncle, taxi?"

"'No, thank you, I am waiting for my driver."

"Where is he taking you?" I was asked above the din. "Agonda," I said cupping one ear with my hand trying to hear him.

"How much will he charge you?" he boldly asked.

I thought for a moment and lied. "Nothing, it's been arranged by my hosts." That did the trick but I had the same conversation again five minutes later with another couple of drivers hoping for a fare.

With the time available to me before my driver would turn up, I wandered over to a dimly lit roadside bar, took a seat inside and had a beer. It was the first since the day before in Mumbai. The bar was very basic and I was the only customer. Being in this surreal place and feeling the onset of my first alcoholic drink for a while created a trippy feeling.

I finished my beer and stood outside with the crowd of taxi drivers. I must have stood out like a sore thumb, in my straw hat and turmeric stained chinos, my white face amongst a sea of dark skinned Goans.

It was now half an hour past my pick up time and I was beginning to think I might have to hire one of those taxi drivers after all. Just then a car pulled up and out got a young man with the look of someone with the weight of the world on his shoulders. He made his way straight to me. This was my pre-arranged taxi to Agonda.

"My Friend's Place?" He asked gruffly.

"Yes," I replied.

"This is not the main entrance," he said. "I have been waiting at the main entrance." No wonder he looked grumpy. I had followed the rest of the crowd to the wrong entrance. Apparently, there was another entrance marked 'Main Entrance'. I apologised, handed over my bag and got into the front seat of the old Lada.

As we pulled away from the noisy station, silence descended upon the car. I spoke first. I apologised again for keeping him waiting and introduced myself.

"CJ," he said curtly, his frown lifting slightly I thought. "My name is CJ."

He spoke some English and after a thawing of the chilly atmosphere I managed to start a conversation, which began with him and his life in Goa. I ascertained that when he wasn't driving his taxi, he fished with his brother who owned a boat in Agonda. They sold their catch to local restaurants. He was married and had a child. He was Hindu.

The 40-minute journey was interesting. CJ was a very careful driver and I felt safe as we made our way through the dark countryside passing along dimly lit roads and through villages flanked by palm trees with white paint on their trunks which reflected the light from our headlamps as we passed. The sky was clear and the stars shone brightly but there was no moon to be seen. At last, a road sign which said Agonda flashed past, hardly legible in the rural lighting,

Carefully crossing a small stream over a dimly lit narrow stone bridge we emerged onto a dusty earthen track lined by single-storey shack like shops and stalls backed by palms.

The stalls were brightly lit with electric light bulbs of various colours hanging from their awnings. A small orange painted Hindu temple with a striking white ornate wooden entrance door stood amongst them. Owners sat outside of their businesses in the balmy evening air. This was the beginning of the main Agonda beach street, which unbeknown to me at the time was never more than 50 metres from the Arabian Sea at any point along its length.

We weaved our way slowly between tourists and wandering cows, some with their young. The street only took a few minutes to drive from end to end.

We finally came to a halt at a lively part of the street towards the southern end. CJ indicated that we had arrived, pointing to an open fronted restaurant with 'My Friend's Place' painted neatly in red on a yellow sign above the entrance. I thanked him, giving a 500 rupee tip. His face brightened immediately. This was about 5 pounds and would go a long way. My Friend's Place would pay him the full fare and charge me when I checked out at the end of my stay.

The restaurant, which was open to the main street, was busy, mainly with Europeans I thought. There must have been thirty tables each with room for up to six people. Most of the tables were occupied. There was a bar at the far end from which a couple of waiters flitted to and fro. At the entrance where I was standing, was an open kitchen with a fish bar. A smouldering grill laden with two large fish cooking in Goan spices scented the air like a couple of joss sticks. The smell was phenomenal and the sight of the food and people drinking cold beer made me desperate to get to my room, drop my bag and get stuck in.

I stood at the entrance with my bag over my shoulder waiting to catch some ones eye. Sure enough the manager owner who had seen me arrive came to greet me. A few heads turned to watch. Clumsily, I put my hands together and mumbled 'namaste' while bowing slightly. The salutation was not returned but a warm welcome was nonetheless given. "Welcome," she said smiling. Her perfect white teeth handsomely contrasted with her dark Goan complexion. Her short slim upright posture complimented a red *sari*, and her intelligent features with black hair combed back into a bun, gave her an air of authority. Indeed over the coming five days that impression would be borne out. "My name is Sita, I am the owner with my husband Ravi. You must be tired after your journey. I will take you to your room then you must come into the restaurant and eat." It felt like a succession of orders and indeed, I felt compelled to obey. After a long day of having to be sensible, it was nice for someone else to take charge.

You should not be surprised when coming to Mumbai or Goa that the namaste salutation is not used as widely as you may imagine. You would be less embarrassed if you were to wait for someone to say it to you, then return the compliment. Simple courtesy and gentle friendliness will suffice. Of course, in other parts of India it may be different, but until I visit them I will not know.

Walking through the busy restaurant trying not to knock people with my bag, I followed Sita into a space with two rows of brightly coloured terraced chalets facing each other with a rough strip of ground separating them by about 20 feet. Each chalet had a sturdy looking entrance door with a big padlock securing it. To the front of each door was balcony space enough for the resident to sit out on a cushioned seat, which was provided. The balcony ran unbroken along the entire length of the five chalets on my side. At the end of the terraces, there were a number of palm trees swaying in the balmy evening breeze with a narrow path running between them. I was later to learn that the path lead to the beach, which was literally a 30 second walk.

There were three low steps leading up to my portion of the balcony and beside them a bowl of water provided for washing your feet prior to entering your chalet. Awkwardly, I removed my shoes and socks, wincing at the pain in my knee as I balanced on my left leg to remove the sock from my right foot. Having dipped each foot into the bowl of water, Sita showed me into my chalet which was basic but clean and welcoming.

As we entered, the first room was the bedroom. The temperature in the room was just right given the lingering heat of the day. There was a large double bed with a white sheet pulled tightly over the mattress.

Two blankets were placed at the end of the bed. I thought I may need them, looking at the large air-conditioning unit high above the headboard. The pillows looked plump and comfortable.

There was a built-in wardrobe and a low table against the wall facing the bed on which to place my bits and pieces. The bathroom like the bedroom was spacious and tiled throughout, it was more of a wet room really with the shower next to the toilet. A grill just above head level opened to the outside allowing light and sounds of the neighbourhood to filter through. I hoped nothing of a creepy crawly nature would come in.

It was as I had imagined, not too tourist orientated. With the bare facilities, you may expect from a beachside chalet in India, it was charmingly basic, and delightfully adequate.

Sita left me to it. I wasted no time in getting myself organised, ready to have a long-awaited beer and something to eat. As I was locking my chalet door, my next-door neighbour came out onto the balcony to sit with a beer in the evening air. I chatted with him for a few minutes. He told me in an Australian accent that he was waiting to leave. His taxi would be picking him up shortly to take him to the airport at Madgoan.

When I had decided to come to India, one of my nagging concerns was spiders. I couldn't find anything to suggest there were big hairy tarantula type creatures in Goa or Mumbai, nevertheless I thought I would ask my neighbour if he knew anything. He told me that as far as he was aware there were no spiders to worry about but that I should be aware that there are snakes and sea snakes. He said that he went for a walk off the beaten track a few days previously and was confronted by an enormous cobra, which startled, had risen up in his path and was displaying its strike pose. He had heard that a cobra could outrun a man if it wanted to but that it probably wanted to stay out of trouble the same as he did.

He described how he slowly backed away and legged it to the main road. "Just be careful and stick to the beaten track, mate," he said. As for sea snakes, it was just something he had been told but hadn't seen any, having spent the best part of his holiday swimming. Reassured, I wished him well and made my way into the restaurant.

Finding a table small enough for one but large enough for two, I ordered a large bottle of Kingfisher larger. I relaxed back and drank quickly. Raising my hand to a passing waiter, I ordered another and drank half of that quite quickly too before settling down into that comfortable place we go to when the alcohol finally finds its way to the brain.

My thoughts soon turned to food. Looking at the menu there was plenty to choose from. As I considered the choices, I sensed something brushing against my left leg. Looking down, it was a small dog sitting close to my leg, a terrier, I think. It had a rusty brown coat and a friendly looking face with large appealing eyes, one brown and the other blue. As I turned my head downwards to look at it, it turned its head away from me quickly as if to avoid eye contact. In doing so however, it moved even closer to my leg and its right shoulder was now pressing quite firmly against my left calf muscle making maximum contact. As I turned my head away from it, it would raise its head again and stare at me. We played this game for a minute or so. It would seem that the young thing just wanted to be friends. It never begged for food once during the five evenings it joined me for dinner and we played the bashful eye thing most times.

I was about to order some food when, with shoulder length auburn curls and flowing evening summer dress, a woman swept smartly into the restaurant. She made straight to the bar and began to speak to Sita. She certainly made an entrance, turning one or two heads with her presence. I discretely observed her speaking to Sita as I drank my beer. They seemed to know each other quite well. The woman was about 5'8". She had a moderately attractive chubby face and was well built but not fat. She was probably in her mid-forties and was definitely European.

As the two women chatted, Sita's husband Ravi came towards my table with a big smile on his face. "Hello, sir, I hope your table is OK for you and that everything is alright with your chalet. Would it be OK if a young lady joined you?" I was struck dumb. Before I could answer, the young lady was standing at the table smiling and pulling the chair opposite me back to prepare to sit down. What could I do? I stood out of courtesy and said 'hello' gesturing her to have the seat, which she had obviously already made her mind up about. Ravi left us. I looked down at the dog, which looked smartly down at the floor again. I wondered if it was in on this?

Since arriving in India I had learned it seemed that everything and everyone seems to be connected. There appeared to be a lot of back scratching going on. Buying something from someone for example will invariably result in them introducing you to someone else who could help with perhaps a taxi somewhere or an introduction to a particular bar or restaurant. How was it, I wondered, that this lady suddenly appeared and was introduced to me within an hour of me arriving? Who's back was being scratched now? I wondered.

I introduced myself and she responded in a strong French accent but with enough English to get by. Her name was Fleur. I learned that she had been living in Agonda for the past three months and was renting a place about two miles from the main Agonda village. She drove here on her scooter.

Out of courtesy I tried to appear interested, however, I was tired and just wanted to relax, eat and drink before falling into bed. Having a conversation with this stranger was something of an effort I did not want to make.

I ordered my food which was King Prawn stir-fried noodles. I thought I would order the delicious smelling fish – which had greeted my nostrils on arrival – another time when I could enjoy it undisturbed. Fleur ordered a light salad because she "'ad eaten earlier." I wondered why she '*ad* bothered coming out for another meal then?

We chatted away as best we could, talking about nothing in particular, pretending to understand one another. After finishing my meal and another couple of drinks, I asked her what she did. She said, "I am a masseur."

"Oh, that's nice," I said. "*Ayurvedic?*"

I don't think she really understood me but said, "oh yes." If she was into *Ayurvedic* therapeutic massage she may have an opinion about my knee. I thought. "How much do you charge for a massage?" I said.

"No, no, I am not that massage," she said in a raised voice, eyes wide open and furrows appearing on her forehead and face flushing slightly under her tanned skin. I realised immediately the stupidity of my question as I quickly lifted my knee from under the table making the dog give a yelp as its comfort was disturbed. Pointing at my knee I explained that I was having trouble and wondered if massage may help. She looked at me dubiously and by now half the restaurant was as well. Things eventually settled down as they do and order was restored. I apologised for making her feel uncomfortable and it would seem all was forgiven. We didn't talk about my knee any more that evening. In actual fact, we didn't talk about very much and in between the silences I wondered why she was even sitting with me and wished she would just go away.

It was late, about midnight, and the restaurant had largely done its business for the night with just a few stragglers enjoying late drinks. I took my leave of Fleur thanking her for her company and headed for bed. The dog was fast asleep under the table.

I slept deeply until 7:30 am. I was woken, I think, by the sound of indistinct chanting from somewhere and the unmistakeable hiss of waves breaking onto the nearby shore. Not quite aware of my surroundings and with a dry mouth from the beer and wine the previous evening, it took a few minutes for me to come to my senses completely. As my awareness grew, so did my excitement and anticipation of what the day may bring.

I hadn't seen the beach yet and with all of the enthusiasm of a young child waking on its first day of a holiday by the seaside, I sprang out of bed 69-year-old style, put on my shorts, a t-shirt and trainers, had a pee, washed my hands and face and cleaned my teeth. I picked up my straw hat and manbag into which I packed my iPod earphones and phone. Most importantly, I filled my Life Straw with water from the sink tap and left the chalet.

The balmy evening air from the previous night was being replaced with growing daytime warmth. The place smelled differently. You could smell the warmth building like you can when an oven has just been switched on and is beginning to heat up.

I decided to step out into the street to have a quick look around before making my way to the beach. I didn't get far before a shopkeeper who was just opening up greeted me.

"Good morning, sir, how are you? Looking for gifts to take home?" he asked. I explained that I had only just arrived and was looking for the beach. He told me his name was Banu and he hoped I would come to him to buy gifts for home when it was time to leave. I said I would.

Banu told me the beach was just 20 yards away and pointed to a sandy path going through a group of palm thatched beach chalets nestling amongst coconut trees. There were a few cows lying around half-awake after a night's sleep. They glanced at me momentarily as I passed and said 'good morning' to them.

As I emerged from the trees and chalets, the beach opened up before me. The smell of the sea and warming sand, along with the aroma of brewing coffee coming from the beach bars as they prepared for the day, was an evocative mix.

A mile of golden sand laid either side of me. A few feet ahead the Arabian Sea moved with nothing more than a gentle swell. Wavelets gently braking onto the pristine shoreline, sand ran rhythmically up the shallowly inclining beach before receding with a hiss as it fell back again into the sea. *These were the sights and sounds of paradise,* I thought.

There were very few people around. Taking advantage of the solitude, I decided to walk for as long as the beach would allow. With my trainers removed, I waded ankle deep along the shore. The water was cool but far from cold. Before long, I decided to go in.

Placing my belongings on a sandy bank and stripping down to my shorts I slowly walked into the sea; it was amazing.

Here I was on my own in India having an early morning swim. I was euphoric and immediately transported back to being 10 years old in Malta where I lived for two years with my parents and two younger siblings. I used to pretend to go to school but spent most of my time playing truant and swimming at the local beach; solitary but happy.

After my swim, I walked along the beach with just my shorts on, allowing them and myself to dry in the morning sun. It was now 9am and the temperature was rising steadily.

Passing along the beach towards me were occasional joggers and at various points along the sandy bank people were practicing their yoga and meditation.

At the end of this stretch of the beach, there was a lagoon. The blue water was perfectly still and reflected the dense palms, which lay behind it. I wondered what might be in that water if I was to take another dip. I recalled the Australian's warning about sea snakes so I put my trainers and shirt back on and carried on walking around the lagoons sandy edge as it made its way inland.

The Agonda village main street which I had seen as I arrived the previous evening gradually came into view as I emerged from the beach.

8. Mini and Nosferatu

I recognised some of the stalls and the little temple I had passed the night before. The stalls and gift shops were open and their owners watched expectantly from the shade of their awnings as tourists strolled slowly by, browsing their goods. Brightly coloured t-shirts, loads of leather sandals, jewellery, and all manner of Indian *objet d'art* were up for grabs at ridiculously low prices. Throughout my stay, I noticed how, despite the rock bottom prices being asked, many tourists were hell bent at getting another 50% off if they could. It is acceptable and indeed expected that you will haggle; however, I thought this behaviour was downright rude.

Walking along, I was drawn to a shop with an attractive display of carved Hindu gods, elephants, tigers and all manner of animals found in India. They were set neatly out on beautiful Kashmiri rugs. Hanging neatly above the display were colourful fine silk scarves and *pashminas*.

A voice came from inside the shop bidding me 'good morning'. I couldn't see anyone as I peered in. As my eyes adjusted to the shade of the shop interior, the voice assumed form. It was a gentleman. He was about 5'6", slim and looked to be about forty. His complexion was lighter than most

Goans and his fine features told me he was either from Pakistan or Kashmir.

Following polite introductions he told me his name was Abdul. He proudly showed me around his shop telling me about the various items he had for sale. I explained that I was just taking a stroll and had only arrived last night, making a point that I wasn't going to buy anything.

It must have been clear to him that he wasn't going to make a sale, however, he invited me to take a seat and have chai and cake with him. He called his assistant and told him to fetch the refreshments. We talked a little about his business and I about my life in England. He told me about his wife and children in Kashmir and how he came to be in Goa. We spoke for what seemed like ages before the tea and cake arrived. *This is my breakfast,* I thought.

The company was delightful with apparently no strings attached at all. An hour had passed and not wishing to outstay his very warm welcome I decided it was time for me to be on my way. "I have enjoyed talking to you, please call again," he said. Thanking him for his hospitality I said goodbye and continued my walk up the high street in the increasingly hot morning sun. *What just happened there?* I thought to myself.

Along the way, shop owners constantly called out with invites of no obligation browsing. They would continue to call for as long as they thought a prospective customer was still in earshot. This was particularly challenging if you happened to stop and look at a stall close to the previous one.

The owner's sales pitch mingled with the shouts and appeals of the previous one was a heady mix. One of the things the lady owners were good at was putting psychological pressure on you. If you showed any interest in an item at all and said something like, "very nice, maybe later." the response would be rapid and forthright. "When?" and "do you promises to come back and buy from me?" That word promise is a powerful one. It challenges your integrity. It also challenges you emotionally especially when the lady is holding a child. Do you say emphatically 'no' or do you lie and say 'yes' when you don't mean it. 'Maybe', won't work. You have already said that.

After my swim, beach walk and shop browsing I was glad to get back to My Friend's Place for a shower and a spot of lunch. The shower was full and forceful. As I enjoyed the warm water washing away the salt and sand from the mornings swim, I noticed something move on a pipe just above my head. Immediately images came to mind of snakes and spiders. From a distance, totally in the buff and covered in shower gel and foam I could see it. It was green, staring at me with two bulging eyes and a broad reptilian head, the sides of which moved in and out as it breathed rhythmically. It was about 4 inches long and two inches wide. A frog. It must have come through the open grill and enjoyed the cool damp atmosphere of the shower room.

I named the frog Mini. I really wasn't sure if it was male or female but I assigned it the gender of female. Mini became my chalet buddy. It was nice but a bit weird to come back at the end of each day and call her name by saying, "Hi Mini, I'm home." Sometimes she would be in my room clinging to the wall.

At other times, she would be sitting on my shelf in the shower room. She would never move when I went in to take something off of the shelf. She would just sit there looking at me. One evening she was on the toilet seat, which was awkward.

Having showered and changed my clothes, I decided that on this first day I would explore the area and take it easy. It was now around midday and I thought a good start would be a beer and a light lunch. My Friend's Place restaurant was very quiet with just a couple of people eating and enjoying a beer. Taking a seat at the same table as last night minus dog, I ordered a beer from the same waiter who served me last night. He was young, perhaps 20. He was about 5'8", slim, with a cheeky smile, which came mainly from his eyes. His head was shaved completely bald, which complimented his dark Goan complexion, as did his perfect white teeth.

He didn't speak much English, however, he obviously felt I was approachable as he took my order and patted me on my own baldhead giving me a wink and another cheeky smile. Slightly embarrassed I smiled back as he went off to get my beer. The beer arrived without further incident and I settled down to drink it and study the lunch menu.

While studying the menu a voice broke my concentration. "Hello." The French accent was familiar. It was Fleur from the night before. She had come to give Sita a massage in return for lunch. She asked if she could join me and have hers now. I said OK.

My King prawn stir-fry was very good. Fleur had salad again. As we talked about this and that, another woman appeared at the table. She knew Fleur and had come across to say hello. Her name was Cloud. She was English and spoke with a slight plum in her mouth I thought.

She seemed to say 'ya' a lot instead of 'yes'. She was slim, about five feet high and had an attractive round face framed by jet-black hair, which I imagined was dyed since she must have been approaching 50. Each time before speaking she breathed in, held her breath and looked up as if for inspiration. Like Fleur, she had been in Goa for the past couple of months. Cloud explained that she was doing past-life regression for anyone who wanted it.

Over the next half an hour we all seemed to get along well. Cloud asked me what I intended to do during my stay. I said I wanted to visit a nature reserve which I had read about, and see some Hindu Temples. I explained that I wanted to hire a taxi driver to take me on a tour to see these things, but for today I was just going to have a look around Agonda.

Fleur told me that there was a very nice place called Palolem just a short tuk-tuk drive away. She said she needed to visit someone there to pay them for something. She said that it would be a good place to visit on my first day and offered to show it to me after she had given Sita a massage. She would go halves on the tuk-tuk fare.

Cloud said that she was doing a past-life regression with a lady from Sweden that afternoon, otherwise she would have come with us. Instead, she asked me if I would like to go to a local music venue for a beer that evening after eating.

There were loads of open mike evenings at various bars in Agonda and being interested in music I said I would like that. Cloud, it turns out had the chalet directly opposite me. Fleur said nothing and just smiled.

Having had lunch I didn't want to hang about for anyone, especially for a girly who wanted to massage someone for an hour. I told Fleur that actually I was keen to get on and would make my own way to Palolem. "No, no," she said in that

French accent. "I will massage Sita later." I wondered how Sita may feel having been let down by her masseur.

"Come," she said, "let's find a tuk-tuk." We said farewell to Cloud who said she would see me later. I sensed that there was a danger here of getting sucked into a social scene which I wished to avoid as a single traveller.

The tuk-tuk ride was scary. I didn't realise just how nippy they were outside of the city. The driver overtook trucks, and passed between them and approaching buses without the slightest hesitation. Cows appeared from nowhere and horns blew constantly. On those roads, a tuk-tuk ride is adrenaline-inducing.

The 20-minute drive seemed less and our arrival in Palolem was a ground kissing moment. Fleur had laughed loudly all the way, occasionally throwing her head back and flinging her arms around like some crazed 1950s movie star in a black and white movie. I braced myself against collision for the whole journey, which made my stomach muscles hurt at the end of it.

Palolem is a much busier place than Agonda. Some say it is inevitable that one day, sleepy Agonda will succumb to the commercialisation of this place. Despite its dusty streets lined each side with tourist shops, cafes and bars Palomas beach scene is one worthy of any luxury holiday film footage.

Lined with iconic coconut palms, beach bars and restaurants, the large pristine sandy beach runs gently into the Arabian sea while fishing and sightseeing boats sit waiting for their moment on its sandy edge.

I suggested to Fleur that she should find her friend and that I would meet her back at our drop off in two hours to share a tuk-tuk back to Agonda. Alternatively she could return to Agonda on her own. I wanted to explore Palolem on my own. Unfortunately, she insisted on accompanying me and said she could call in on her friend on the way back.

Two hours turned into five. Fleur left me at a beach side bar and went off to pay her debts, returning half an hour later. I was now able to rest my very sore and swollen knee. In a way, I was glad I was able to complain about my knee given the previous night's conversation about the price of a massage.

The return journey was even more hair raising as darkness descended quite quickly. Horns and dodgy manoeuvres were now accompanied by flashing lights interspersed with pitch-black darkness as we drove along the country roads. I remember thinking about cows. How would we ever see one in the middle of the road in time? It worked out, however, as I am sure it always did.

When we got back, Fleur said goodbye and disappeared to find Sita. I went back to my chalet for a freshen-up before going into the restaurant for a beer and some food. I was glad to be on my own again and wasn't really looking forward to going to a music venue with Cloud, a relative stranger.

There was fresh barbequed Goan style fish, on the menu that evening at My Friends Place. As I entered the restaurant the delicate aroma of spices and exotic pastes being infused into the bodies of the whole fish on the grills instantly stimulated my appetite.

This is what I wanted tonight, I thought. The grill bar was open to the street, as was the restaurant, and the aromas and beautiful display of freshly caught fish drew the attention of every passer-by on their early evening stroll.

I was beckoned over with a wave from one of the grill chefs to view the beautiful display of fish. I chose a whole Goan bream to be grilled in South Indian spices, accompanied by char grilled vegetables.

The strange waiter who also was present at the fish grill acknowledged me with his cheeky smiley eyes wide open, eyebrows raised as if in expectation and proceeded to walk around the back of me and deeply massage my shoulders near my neck.

The two chefs working at the grill who had seen what was happening smiled lightly as they carried on with their cooking. Now I love having my shoulders massaged but this was bazar. Releasing myself from his grip with a little dip and body twist I gave a polite laugh and asked him if I could have a large beer. He patted my head again and went off to fetch it. *This cannot go on,* I thought, as I made my way back to my table. Thankfully someone else appeared with my beer.

This was my second night in Agonda and as I enjoyed my beer and anticipated my meal, I reflected on the events of the past 24 hours. I recalled my journey from the train station to Agonda and the hospitality of the Kashmiri shop owner this first morning. The arrival of Fleur during my first evening meal was really strange; and Cloud, appearing during lunch, offering to accompany me to a music venue this evening was crazy.

The dog, which I had now named Rudyard, was once again, sitting with his little wiry shoulder firmly pressed against my leg under the table, avoiding eye contact again as if he had something to hide.

The fish which I had ordered was delicious but some of the vegetables were a little firm for my liking. The charring from the grill made them look good though. I had great expectations about the food in India, but so far, I had mixed feelings and felt a little disappointed. I had no doubt that the perfect Indian meal had yet to reveal itself.

It was now around 9 pm and the night was coming alive. Music from neighbouring bars drifted into the street and people, a mix of European and Asian, were out and about enjoying the Agonda nightlife. Cloud turned up just as I finished my meal and we went to a bar nearby called Oasis.

There was a solo artist, a European girl playing guitar and singing. She was utilising some electronic backing music and effects, which softened and partially covered her shrill voice. The special effects were the main element of the songs she performed.

One of the annoying things that happen in Agonda and presumably in Goa generally is a power cut. Every so often – that is four or five times each night – the electricity stops. The result of this for the performer was catastrophic. Her voice and mastery of the guitar were laid bare, often for periods of a minute or more in between power ups. The poor creature died on stage at least twice that night.

Cloud was fairly quiet and I realised quite quickly that we didn't really have much in common to talk about. I just wanted to leave and sit somewhere quiet with a beer so I said I was going to do just that and wished her good night. "I'll come with you," she said. *Oh, for God's sake,* I thought.

Walking a few yards down the street on my way back to My Friend's Place I found a quiet bar with vacant tables outside in the warm evening air. Without asking Cloud if she thought it was OK, I walked in and took a table. She followed and sat opposite me. I had nothing to say really so remembering what she had said about her stay in Agonda, I asked her to tell me a little about past life regression. That was it. She never stopped talking.

After a fairly tiring evening discussing previous lives and those to come, I was ready to return to My Friend's Place and have a nightcap before retiring. Since Cloud lived there too we walked back together.

Upon our arrival, the smiling weird waiter, Sita, and Fleur greeted us. "Come, sit," said Sita in a serious voice with little emotion on her face. I wondered if something was wrong. She beckoned Cloud and I to join her and Fleur at a table near the bar. The waiter hovered around our table flexing his fingers as if to play a piano or perhaps pounce on me again. He had a big wide-eyed evil smile and was looking directly at me. Sita who was his boss and employer told him to leg it. To my relief he did, looking back at me over his shoulder as he left with that wide-eyed grin which reminded me of Nosferatu disappearing into the night to look for another victim.

There was nothing wrong. Sita was simply gathering her friends around her for a catch-up after a busy day. It was now past midnight and I just had to sleep. They asked me what I was up to the next day and I said that I was going to have some time to myself on the beach. I hoped that would send a clear message.

It was Fleur this time that invited me to join her at a beach bar called Arabian Nights after my day at the beach following dinner. I thought about it for a few seconds then agreed since I thought it might be nice to have a bit of company later in the evening.

Before I took myself off to bed, I mentioned to Sita that I was keen to visit the nature reserve and see some Hindu temples at some point. I wondered how I might go about that. "I will arrange it for you for the day after tomorrow," she said. "It will cost 6000 rupees and I will come with you. It will be a very long day."

I couldn't believe it. I just wanted to be on my own. I thanked her anyway and made my way to bed. *What did these people want?* I thought to myself as I fumbled with the key to my padlocked chalet.

9. Monkeys, Dogs and Arabian Nights

The next morning I woke at around 7 am and made my way to the beach for a swim and this time some meditation, which helped ground me and lay the foundation for my day. It felt good to be on my own again, as I walked along the beach drying off in the warming morning sun. I remember thinking of home and the rain and wind that was currently battering the south of England.

The walk was in the opposite direction along the beach this day. Stopping at a beachside bar I had chai but nothing to eat. It felt cleansing to go without breakfast and just feel nourished by the sweet cardamom tea. The natural high I was now experiencing from my early morning swim and meditation was increased by this relaxing interlude sipping the tea and staring out at the Arabian sea, soft foam running up the beach and the sun rising, spreading its warmth. I remember connecting with my breath and taking it all in with a sense of wonder.

After my chai breakfast, I continued to walk along the beach to its southernmost end where beach met forest. Once again, remembering my neighbours warning about snakes I kept fairly close to the beaten track. I was on my own now as

I passed tall palm trees with coconuts waiting to fall, and thick bushes concealing goodness knows what. There was a path, which led off from the one I was on. It went into the forest of trees, palms and bushes. I decided to be brave and cautiously follow it into the forest just a little way. I had gone about 50 metres when I heard a rustling of the foliage above me in the trees. Looking up I could see at least a dozen monkeys. I now know that they were a type of macaque called a bonnet monkey. I took my phone out of my manbag, and placed the bag on the ground at my feet. Delighted, I proceeded to take shots of the macaques. I was sure that they were watching me. I stood mesmerised for a while feeling so pleased that at last I had seen some wildlife when suddenly they started to climb down. Slowly at first then gathering speed they were gone from the tree and down on the ground somewhere beyond sight. I could hear their excited chatter and saw the bushes moving frantically ahead of me. *Shit,* I thought as I imagined being set upon. I froze, wondering if I should get out of there fast. I decided that was the sensible thing to do while there was still time. Turning on my heels I made a quick exit from the bush and felt relieved to be back on the main path. Unfortunately in my haste to get away, I had forgotten to pick up my manbag. I had to get it back.

My wallet was in there with my bank and credit cards.

The monkeys were now quite noisy, screeching at each other by the sounds of it. I had visions of one of them with my bag slung over its shoulder proudly prancing around in front of its friends like some hipster from Hackney.

I had no choice, if I didn't recover my bag and its contents I was in trouble. I could feel the fear rising as I gingerly entered the forest again towards the spot where I had seen the monkeys. The screaming had stopped now. Looking up, there was no sign of them in the trees. I wondered where they were and speculated that they may be hiding in the bushes waiting to pounce. As I approached the spot, to my relief, I spotted my bag. It was still closed and looked in one piece. With no sign of monkeys, I dashed forward and retrieved it. It was, I suppose, an emotionally primordial experience being in the wild and in competition with animals. In a way, a struggle for survival. Them, watching out for their territory, and me, another primate, protecting my belongings, which were of great importance for my well-being and security.

When I got back to the path, I hurriedly checked my bag for its contents, especially to see if all of my cards were still there. It occurred to me afterwards how ridiculous the thought was of a monkey opening my bag and going through my wallet, selectively taking out my cards and checking the expiry dates. I laughed as I pictured myself reporting the theft to the local police, trying to give a description.

The walk back to My Friend's Place was leisurely, my knee was swollen and sore now and I was ready for a rest. Upon my return, I found that Sita had made arrangements for my tour the next day. She had arranged the taxi with CJ, my airport driver, and he was to meet me at the restaurant at 8 am. Apparently, he had put together a schedule, which would take in the whole day. We would be back for 7 pm. Apologising, Sita said she would not be able to come after all. I was glad; this was my tour and I didn't want to have to make friendly chitchat and think about someone else all day.

After taking a refreshing shower with Mini peering at me from her pipe above my head, I made my way into the restaurant for some lunch and an early beer. Lunch was my favourite stir-fry and the beer made me relaxed and sleepy.

When I had finished, I went back to my chalet and had a snooze. It was too hot to lie around on the beach in the afternoon sun and 4 pm was the best time to head for the beach. The sun set at around 6:30. With a spectacular sunset, it was the place to be for an early evening beer before getting ready for dinner and some nightlife.

It was now about 3:30 and following my siesta I made my way to the beach for a relaxing swim and sunbathe. As with the previous few days, the weather was beautiful and the water warm and inviting.

I savoured the next couple of hours on the beach before being joined by Cloud. It was not a busy beach and I must have been easy to spot. I only knew she was there when she sat down beside me on the sand and tapped my arm.

She asked if I would like to go for a sundowner. The bar was right on the edge of the beach. It was a truly beautiful sunset. The beauty of it all accentuated by a second bottle of beer.

Just as the large red sun kissed the horizon, a horse and rider passed in front of it on the shoreline. My phone at the ready the moment was captured forever.

We watched until the sun disappeared then strolled back the short way to My Friend's Place. I returned to my chalet for a shower and change of clothes before the evening meal and Cloud went for a lie-down saying she had a headache. I was sorry about the headache but glad that I would be eating on my own that evening. I had built up a good appetite.

As I enjoyed my meal of mixed fish grill, I noticed that Rudyard wasn't beside me. Normally he would see me come into the restaurant and pad over to his usual spot beneath my table.

I was just coming to the end of my meal when there was a commotion outside in the dusty street. It was the sound of dogs barking and howling. Just then, Sita's husband, Ravi, came over to me with a big grin on his face. "Come see," he said. I stood up and went with him to the entrance of the restaurant. Looking out onto the dusty rickety road I could see that there were around ten dogs of various breeds barking and howling at one solitary black, grey whiskered dog standing his ground and quietly staring them down. The dog was the size of a Labrador but was scrawny and looked as if he had been in many a good scrap. The scene reminded me of a cowboy film where the bad man comes to town and stands in the middle of the street waiting for a gun fight. I was in the saloon looking out.

The pack of howling mutts were about 30 feet from the dog. The tension was building and I could see it was all going to kick off quite soon. The black dog was silent and steadfast just staring at the barking, snarling pack, which were now displaying their teeth. Whenever the dog shifted its position, for no other reason than comfort, the mob would advance a few feet, bark hysterically, and back off again. Regardless, he stood there, cool, silent and measured, as the pack went wild. Then, in a breath holding moment of tension, slowly, he made his way forward. Bravely, fearlessly step-by-step he moved towards them. Head down, shoulders hunched, with body low, he was going to take each one of them on and they knew it. Suddenly with one last joint enormous howl and growl, they turned tail, and with the exception of one wire-haired terrier, they ran away.

My heart sank. It was Rudyard! He was giving it everything he had, not realising, I suspect, that the other pack members had run off and left him to it. Now in terms of size matching bravery, Rudyard was as fearless as the black dog but less than half its size. This was a one-on-one shoot-out and Rudyard didn't stand a chance.

By now, there were around a hundred spectators viewing from both sides of the street in silence wondering what would happen next. But Ravi had seen it all before and ran out to break it up. Rudyard ran back into the restaurant and hid under my table while the black dog coolly turned and walked off. Rudyard's bravery made me well up. I do a lot of that these days for the silliest of reasons but especially after a couple of beers.

Following my meal and the excitement of the canine stand-off, I made my way to the Arabian Nights beach bar to meet Fleur as arranged. When I arrived, the place was already lively with groups of Europeans sitting around drinking and loud music playing. I ordered a beer and waited at the bar. The place was very well-situated, overlooking the beach with the sea just behind it. I could just make out the sound of foaming water running up the beach with each small breaker and the hissing it made upon its return to the sea. It was warmly lit and there were softly cushioned bamboo sofas and chairs placed strategically around. The best seats I thought were on the terrace, which overlooked the beach. A fantastic spot to watch the sunset if you were there early enough to get a seat.

Leaning on the bar I casually sipped my beer biding my time, when an arm came around my shoulder and dragged on it and my neck. The woman who was either on drugs or was drunk or both had her face two inches from mine. She wanted me to come and meet her friends and join them all for a drink. I thanked her for the offer but declined, citing the imminent arrival of my friend. "Come on, don't be a spoilsport," she said in a Scandinavian accent, her arm tightening around my shoulder. She was slim, tanned, attractive and blond. She must have been in her late thirties. In retrospect, I feel she could have been sent by some Hindu deity to test my ego. There was no temptation and the experience was unpleasant.

Eventually, Fleur arrived, saving me from this persistent pest who gave her a look of distaste and left to join her friends. We had a beer and chatted as best we could, given her strong French accent and me speaking no French at all. The evening was pleasant enough drinking and listening to the music.

I was conscious of the next day's tour and the early start so I decided to stop drinking and go back to my chalet for a reasonably early night. I left Fleur chatting to some people she knew. I felt there was much I didn't know or understand about her but with just two days left in Goa she would remain a mystery.

10. The Tour

I had a good night's sleep waking at 7 am to prepare myself for the day ahead. After greeting Mini and showering, I gathered my belongings for the day. My Life Straw, which was filled with water from the shower-room tap and everything else I needed, fitted snugly into my manbag.

It was going to be a long hot day so I wore my light chinos, which had since been laundered for me by the chalet maid. My trainers and cheesecloth short-sleeved shirt ensured I would be comfortable for the rest of the day. My straw trilby was a constant companion.

Breakfast in the restaurant was chai and a toasted bun with cheese. As I sat waiting for CJ to arrive, I reflected on the previous night and wondered what awaited me in the coming last two days.

CJ arrived promptly. His little Taxi with air-conditioning had been spruced up by the looks of things. He had provided water and there was a box of tissues on the dashboard. He was in a better mood than when he met me at the rail station by the look of him.

We set off at around 8 am leaving Agonda behind for the day. It was something of a relief really. I had unwittingly become involved with people and felt slightly constrained by them. I decided that on my next visit to India I probably wouldn't stay in one place longer than two days.

The day trip would take us inland initially, then north before making our way slowly south again to Agonda. After travelling for 30 minutes through small villages and scrubland we arrived at the Sri Shantadurga Fatarpekarin Temple. The temple was established in the 1500s and is dedicated to around a dozen deities. It is a spectacular large complex, which had been added to over the centuries. Decorated in red and cream plasterwork it contrasted beautifully against the surrounding forest. Apparently, the festivals of which there are many are vibrant, colourful and spectacular.

CJ and I went through the entrance taking our shoes off first. It was a very warm morning and the cool marble floor felt wonderful on my bare feet.

The temple consisted of a large white marble floored area probably the size of a tennis court. On each side was a pillared walkway. The pillars were faced with marble and had ornate capitals supporting a balcony above, which presumably was accessible to worshippers.

Ahead of us and at the end of the great hall was a smoothly plastered light green wall with white plastered boarders forming an archway in its centre. The archway was decorated with carvings of elephants and deities which had garlands of fresh bright orange flowers draped around their stone necks. The archway led somewhere which looked to be some sort of vestry. It was not accessible to worshippers as there was a beautifully carved brown, stained-wooden balustrade extending the whole width of the building in front of it. It struck me how similar the layout was to a Christian church except that there were no pews, only the occasional chair here and there for those unable to sit on the marble floor.

Again, not unlike a Christian church, at the ringing of a bell the Hindu priest would emerge with holy sacraments consisting of water, fire and rice. Worshippers approached and ritualistically received these. First moving the hands quickly and cautiously through the flames of the fire offered to them as if scooping it up. The water was offered into their hands from a ladle then they were given rice. This symbolic ritual was repeated regularly throughout the day.

I was encouraged by CJ to approach the balustrade and have a closer look at the archway with its carvings, which I did. While gazing at the beautifully decorated deities, a bell rang and a priest came out of the archway bringing with him fire, water and bread.

I found myself standing with other members of the congregation who were dropping money into a basket held out by the priest then receiving first fire then water followed by rice. I was in one of those don't know what to do situations but before long the priest got to me and held out the basket and I put 250 rupees in it. The priest stood there with his fire, water and rice. I turned and looked at CJ, he nodded at me, eyebrows raised, as if to say 'go on, hurry up get on with it'. So I did, scooping up the fire, then not knowing what to do with the water the priest had put into my hands proceeded to drink it. The rice came next which I ate.

With embarrassment, I walked away from that balustrade feeling stupid and annoyingly, badly advised by CJ. I saw two old boys sitting on their chairs observing me and smiling.

I tried to apologise for any embarrassment caused to CJ for my awkward actions in the temple but he just shrugged his shoulders and said it was OK. I wanted him to say 'no absolutely nothing to apologise for' but he didn't have that much English and I got the impression that he didn't have much patience either. At least not with me.

Leaving Fatorpa, the temple, and my embarrassment, we drove on a further 30 minutes down the road to a small town called Quepem. We stopped outside of what looked like another Hindu temple but turned out to be a building erected in that style in 1787 by a Portuguese nobleman. It is called the Palacio Do Deao. We didn't go in.

We drove on and were about 50 km away from Agonda. It was now around 10:30 and after passing through small villages and scrub land with the occasional wandering cow, and small monkey sitting by the roadside staring at us as we passed by, we crossed the river Ragada before stopping at the ancient Mahadeva temple at Tambdisurla.

This was a really interesting place dedicated to Lord Shiva and built in the 13 century AD. There were plenty of tourists looking around but they looked to be mainly Indian.

The temple was a very serene place to visit. It is situated in the Western Ghats or hills, and sits amongst green woodland supported by slowly flowing streams.

Built from basalt it is predominantly black which lends a sense of mystery and a little menace in my mind to it. The temple is embellished with carvings of elephants, lotus flowers, and to add to its menace there is an intricate carving of a King Cobra set into the rock inside which is very dimly lit with an even more dimly lit shrine to Shiva deeper within. Legend has it that there is a huge cobra resident in its dimly lit interior.

Emerging into the light and adjusting my eyes I saw that a coach had arrived with around fifty or so school kids. They were all smartly dressed and looked as if they were about 12 or 13. Before long, they were exploring the temple grounds waiting to be shown inside by their guide. Phones were out and pictures were being taken. I noticed that a group of about a dozen boys and girls were looking my way and pushing each other laughing in my direction.

I guessed what would come next as I heard "Uncle, Uncle." They wanted photos with this odd-looking European with a straw hat. I obliged and this went on throughout my walk around the grounds of the temple. At one point, while my ego was at its highest due to the attention I was receiving, I announced to CJ laughingly that I felt like some sort of movie star. I don't think he was impressed. He managed to find the English to tell me unsmiling that I was a novelty. A European who would no doubt be on Instagram in no time and the brunt of their young jokes at school for a few days to come, I thought. I calmed down and got back into the car before being driven off to a spice farm 20 km up the road for lunch and a guided tour.

I thought about the events of that morning and wondered what impression CJ had got of me. The fact that he was always fairly quiet and didn't smile or say much made me wonder about my conduct. I decided I would be more sober in his presence. I liked him and thought he showed wisdom. I felt I needed to show I respected him, which I did.

The spice farm was at a place called Ponda. CJ said he would not come in with me and that he would rest in his car and wait. He told me to take as long as I wished and that I should eat there.

The entrance ticket was only £4 and that included a herbal drink, lunch and a tour. It was a lovely place with palm leaved roofs over the outside dining area with a food counter serving all manner of hot and spicy vegetarian dishes and bread.

Smiling *sari*-wearing ladies served the food, spooning out whatever you wanted from the wide selection on display. The food was the best I had tasted since arriving in India. Pulses and dals with freshly baked bread washed down with a cool herbal drink served in jugs.

Following lunch it was possible to join a guided group to take you around the plantation. This was included with your entry fee. I was about to join one of these groups when I was approached by an Indian lady who suggested that she could give me a personalised tour of the farm which would be a much better experience.

Her name was Lucy. She was about 5-foot tall, of medium build with a pleasant round face complimented by a bright red bindi and an infectious smile. She wore a simple shift dress, which looked less fussy and more comfortable than some of the *sari* wearing staff around and about.

True to her word Lucy gave a very good explanation of all of the various plants and spices. Amongst the most interesting were the cashew and betel nut trees. The cashew, I learned, was poisonous unless cooked. From its kernel, strong clear liquor was distilled. The betel nut was a mild narcotic when chewed and had the effect of a large whisky. Chewing this nut was legal in India. You wouldn't want to swallow too much of the red juice it produced since it would upset your stomach. It was common to see some partakers spitting out its red liquid onto the street in some places. Pretty gross really.

We attended a demonstration of the harvesting of the betel nut. A young man, obviously extremely fit clambered like lightening about 30 feet up one of these trees, pulling the nuts from its canopy before swinging back and forward creating a pendulum effect, then leaping from it to the neighbouring tree. Descending the tree at twice the speed the man arrived on the ground to a round of applause, heaps of rupee notes being thrown into the battered biscuit tin at his feet in appreciation.

As we moved on, Lucy explained that she was a volunteer at the spice farm and that she relied on contributions to provide for herself and her family. I had already intended to give her a tip but appreciated her need to emphasise the importance of doing so.

It was an interesting tour and I enjoyed Lucy's explanations about the plantation. As we walked back to the reception area, I tipped her with Rs 500, which she seemed to be very grateful for. I wasn't looking for gratitude; just an indication that my tip was enough for the 45 minutes I had of her time.

It was a really hot day and on the way out of the tour, the guides leading their groups out of the plantation invited each of them to have a refreshing ladle of ice-cold water poured down their neck. It looked pretty inviting but at the same time scary to hear the screams and see people dancing on the spot to the shock of it. Their clothes soaked but drying quickly in the heat of the day. Apparently, it was good for the heart and circulation.

As the party in front finally passed through this rite of passage it was my turn with the help of Lucy who without warning poured the ice-cold water over the back of my neck. It took my breath away and I couldn't help letting out an expletive or two under my breath. Lucy laughed and assured me that this would prolong my life. My wet chinos took me back to Heathrow and my sink accident.

To complete my tour, Lucy took me to the restaurant and offered me a sample of the liquor made from the cashew kernel. She gave me a very generous glass of this clear liquid. I cautiously took a sip and found it to be pleasant tasting but definitely in the 40% alcohol range. We sat chatting as I sipped my way through the liquor, but before long Lucy spied another potential customer and she was off.

Now slightly high from the liquor I made my way out to the car park where CJ was asleep in the driving seat with one foot resting on the dashboard and the other out of the open window. He must have been very tired in this heat and particularly after all of this driving. He woke as I approached the car giving a polite cough.

We were now heading north and bound for Old Goa. Along the way was the Shri Sausthan Manguesh Temple complex, which was established around 1560 AD. This was a terrible time for the indigenous people of Goa. The Portuguese destroyed many temples in an attempt to stamp out idolatry and establish Christian churches. This one survived.

The temple complex was an extremely busy place and in the baking hot sun it was physically quite challenging climbing the 100 or more steps to its entrance. The long street leading to the steps was lined both sides with market stalls selling refreshments and other useful things for worshippers and tourists. It was a colourful site, busy and noisy. CJ and I didn't go into the temple but wandered around its grounds and the market place for 20 minutes before heading back to the car. It was a relief to get back and escape the heat. My knee was also painful now after wandering around and climbing the steps.

Travelling 40 minutes north we arrived at Old Goa which was Portugal's former capital in India It was 4 pm as we arrived at this fairly busy town with its Catholic cathedral.

CJ invited me to explore the cathedral but I wasn't that keen. After having seen the brightly decorated temples of south Goa, the cathedral looked quite dower. Nevertheless, I thought I would look out of courtesy.

It was a typical Catholic church. The walls adorned with a suffering Christ here and there and saints painted on canvass and walls looked miserable in this dark cavernous place. There was a long line of people curiously filing past these grotesque scenes. I was amongst them. If they were Hindu, I wondered what they thought of Christianity and its depressive symbolism.

As I emerged from that dark place, I was once again approached for a photograph. This time it was a young lady probably 20 or so. "Excuse me, Uncle, selfie photo with you please?" I obliged and she reciprocated for my own collection.

It was now getting on for 5 pm. It had been a long hot full day and I felt that I had achieved pretty much everything I set out to do. We had an hour and a half drive ahead of us now heading south to Agonda. Just as with any other country at this time of the day it was going home time and the traffic was heavy.

The main route we had taken was a fairly major highway. Apart from getting held up briefly by construction works building a highway direct to Mumbai, we made good progress.

I could see that the day had taken its toll on CJ. He was heavy eyed and it was difficult to engage him in conversation, which is what I thought I ought to do to keep him awake. We eventually saw the signs for Agonda and before long we were driving over the little bridge leading into the main Agonda beach rickety road and pulling up outside of My Friend's Place.

I thanked CJ for a great day and paid what I owed him plus a very large tip. He looked happier than at any other time that day. I guessed that money must have been a continual struggle for him and his young family. I remembered what that was like from times past. It dominates your thoughts and eats away at you. Some westerners would try to capitalise on this and haggle aggressively over the fare let alone give a tip. I calculated that CJ earned around £8 an hour that day which was still not the national minimum hourly wage in the UK. I hated the way that some westerners treated the Indian people. Taking advantage of their circumstances and treating them as if they were stupid.

It had been a long day and I was glad to have a shower and go into the restaurant for a beer and a meal. For the next two nights, I ate with Fleur and Cloud at their insistence. Tomorrow was to be my last night and they suggested we do something special. There was a talent night at one of the bars with a seafood BBQ Without thinking, I said I thought that was a great idea and agreed enthusiastically. I had let go of the idea of solitude and had succumbed instinctively to the social animal within.

Tonight was an opportunity to chill after a busy tiring day, so after the meal we just sat around chatting and drinking until it was time for sleep. I didn't mention what I would be doing on my last full day and hoped I wouldn't be asked. I wasn't, and it worked out well with a day to myself, having beach time and generally relaxing.

That last evening was truly memorable and I remember feeling grateful on this occasion that I had company. There was some good talent at the music venue and the BBQ was lovely. Freshly caught fish grilled and served whole on a palm leaf with rice or potato made a complete meal. Large prawns cooked over charcoal had a lovely smoky sweetness about them and complimented the fish.

The evening soon passed and I decided to finish it off with a nightcap at My Friend's Place before turning in. CJ wasn't picking me up for the airport until 1 pm the next day so there was no hurry to go to bed. It was just as well since I didn't retire until well after midnight.

11. Ebony and Ivory

Despite my late night, I was awake at 7 am. This time with a hangover so I decided to take a last dip in the Arabian Sea. It was as usual; beautifully warm and the sun rising slowly in the morning sky provided me with a perfect farewell to Goa.

After I had my dip, I walked along the beach for the last time and reflected on the peace, which I had found in Agonda. I recalled my experiences since arriving in India, and smiled at some of them. In a small way, I was proud that I had come to this place through my own efforts and organisation. It was this reflection, which made me decide to write about my experiences. The exercise would be purely for my own records but may just be of interest to family or friends in the future. A record of something 'uncle' had done all those years ago.

Returning to my chalet in my damp sandy shorts and t-shirt, I stripped off and made for the shower. I wanted to say a last farewell to Mini but she wasn't there. *Probably out finding her breakfast,* I thought.

Breakfast was congenial, Sita joined me. The waiter who had haunted me for the last few days was working this morning, smiling menacingly at me as he waited on us both.

I guess Sita joining me for breakfast was her diplomatic way of giving me the final bill. As we chatted and drank our chai she slowly slid the bill across the table for me to read 'at my leisure'. It was a faithful record of all of my purchases in the restaurant and in the bar. The accommodation had already been paid through the online booking site. For five days of delicious lunches and evening meals with unfettered use of the bar it was ridiculously cheap. I paid for my food and drink in cash, as everyone liked. Sita implored me to study the bill carefully but I was very happy to pay whatever she had calculated without question and I told her so. She seemed pleased with this.

After breakfast, I walked next door to Banu's shop and bought what amounted to around 40 pounds worth of gifts. This was quite a lot of money really and he seemed delighted that I had kept my word and done my shopping with him. We said our goodbyes and he wished me well, hands together as in prayer with a light bow. I reciprocated this time without awkwardness.

Upon my return to my chalet, there was still no sign of Mini I was disappointed and felt unloved but then realised how ridiculous I was being. "It's a frog for God's sake," I said to myself, and got on with strategically packing my rucksack.

Unlike a suitcase, you have to make sure your rucksack is packed in the correct order. What needs to be accessed in the next 12 hours needs to be packed last and don't put things in there that you will need once the bag has been taken from you at the airport.

I made sure that I had my passport, visa, wallet and phone in my manbag. I also kept my Life Straw in there, which could have been dodgy since taking bottles containing liquids on board was not allowed in the UK. Surprisingly it was OK for my internal flight from Madgoan to Mumbai.

Bag packed and one last look around calling, "goodbye Mini," I made my way to the restaurant for a last beer and stir-fry before my pick up with CJ at 1 pm.

They were all there. CJ who was very early, Sita and her husband Ravi, Fleur, Cloud and the crazy waiter. As I walked in, they invited me to join them at a table presumably set aside for us all. Once again, the crazy waiter was given a look from Sita and he disappeared to get drinks for the table.

Instead of my usual stir-fry, Sita had arranged for vegetarian bites to be served. They included samosas, savoury breads and biscuits and fresh yoghurt dips. I felt absolutely honoured. Since my arrival in India I had been treated with courtesy and kindness. These people who wouldn't leave me alone offered nothing other than unconditional friendship. My final hour in Agonda had been made very special and I was humbled.

After lunch was eaten and the last of the beer swallowed down, it was time to say cheerio. The usual telephone numbers were exchanged and final photographs were taken.

Hugs and farewells were made and as I turned for the last time to say cheerio before getting into the taxi with CJ, my eyes were drawn to the bar where the crazy waiter stood with a wide-eyed ear to ear grin showing his perfect white teeth doing that piano finger thing at me. I nodded at him and got into the taxi waving a final goodbye. We had only moved a few feet when CJ brought the taxi to a halt and smiled at me. Sitting on the sidewalk was Rudyard. I don't suppose he saw me but I gave him a wave and we drove off.

The journey to the airport allowed me to see what I had missed upon my arrival in the dark. The area out of Agonda was forest-like and covered thickly with palms and other trees and foliage. I saw low walls fronting ramshackle houses with chickens and other animals in their yards. There were monkeys sitting on walls beside the road, some of them mothers carrying their young. The weather was once again beautiful and the temperature was now at a very warm 32 degrees. CJ had the air-conditioning on but still invited me to open a window if I wished. I accepted the offer. I remember thinking how lovely it would be to be back in the sea at that moment.

The journey to Madgoan airport was about an hour and CJ's excellent driving made it very pleasant. After half an hour or so, greenery gave way to tarmac and urban sprawl. Airport signs appeared and it was clear that very soon I would be saying goodbye to CJ and Goa.

Pulling gently into the drop-off zone at Madgoan airport CJ, jumped out and got my bag. I thanked him for his very professional driving and his contribution to a very enjoyable stay in Agonda. I tipped him generously and he left with a wave and a smile.

The process of check-in was quite straightforward except that in addition to scanning there was a thorough body search, which was carried out by what appeared to be a soldier.

The wait at the departure gate was just under two hours. There was a bookshop and a bar and well-maintained frequently cleaned toilets. Television screens dotted about the lounge were showing reports of President Modi addressing some sort of rally in Delhi. There were breaking news reports appearing on the bottom of the screen. You didn't need to understand Hindi to see they were about the Covid-19 infection and speculation that there was going to be a pandemic.

The fight from Madgoan to Mumbai was with Spice Jet. It was a fairly small aircraft and appeared to be completely full. Just as with my arrival at Madgoan railway station all announcements were in the various dialects of Hindi as well as English and took some time. I wondered how long it would take for 'brace, brace' to be announced.

The flight was uneventful. It was only an hour to Mumbai and no sooner had we taken off, it seemed we were being asked to buckle up again for landing. I was glad to have taken the train to Goa, as there really was nothing to see of the countryside in that aluminium tube at thirty thousand feet.

I had a window seat and it was dark by the time we landed. As we made our approach, I could see the red taillights of what must have been thousands of vehicles snaking their way for miles on the major roads below me making their way out of the city perhaps. In the opposite direction, presumably coming into the city, were the white headlights from an equal number of vehicles. The sight reminded me of a long string of rubies set against another of diamonds. I wondered if this was going home from work traffic and how long it would take me to get back to my residency in Fort.

The arrival process of travelling internally by air was quick and straightforward. Get off the plane, walk to the carousel, pick up your bag and leave the airport. No document checks whatsoever. Much the same as internal arrivals in the UK I guess but it did surprise me for some reason. I imagined there would be more bureaucracy.

I made my way outside to the passenger arrivals pick up point and looked for my taxi driver who would be holding up my name. The sounds and aromas of Mumbai met my senses again with a rush. The difference between it and Agonda made me realise how peaceful the last five days had been.

Despite the tranquillity I had left behind, I was pleased to be back in the city and looked forward to making the most of my last two days in India.

Looking along the long row of drivers waiting to meet their customers, I saw my name neatly written on a board which was held up chest height by a smiling, smart looking gentleman. He must have been about 65. His lighter complexion told me he was probably from these parts. His white teeth complimented his brown skin. He was slim, about 6 feet and had slightly greying hair, which was wiry and neatly cut. He wore a checked short-sleeved shirt, long trousers and open sandals. Men in Mumbai didn't seem to wear shorts.

He introduced himself as Rudra and taking my bag invited me to follow him to his car, which was parked on the side of the airport road. He must have known that my aircraft had landed and decided to save him and probably me the parking fee.

The car was an old Citroen, which had seen better days. The front inside door panel on my side wasn't attached to the door securely. The window winder and door pull handle were holding it on. My seat had a broken spring, which dug into my left buttock and something was making a rubbing sound, which increased in frequency as we drove off and gathered speed. I speculated that it might be some bodywork rubbing on a tyre or perhaps something going around in the engine compartment about to fail.

Rudra was unperturbed. Very jolly and keen to practice his English he began the conversation with, "Do you like Stevie Wonder?" "Oh, yes," I said. That was all he wanted to hear as he took a tape cassette and inserted it into his on-board sound system consisting of a 1970s Goodman's cassette recorder, which had been attached to the dashboard in front of him with black masking tape. The speaker was somewhere in the back of the car and there were leads trailing from the player to the speaker which were taped along the roof above his door.

The first tune was 'I Just Called'. Rudra burst into song, singing along with it with sincerity and energy. "You like to sing?" He asked. "Well, yes I do," I said and joined in. It was bazar yet at the same time it felt quite natural. Two men in their late sixties who had never met before singing along together to Stevie Wonder. The songs kept coming and the journey to Fort was whizzing by accompanied by 'Superstition', 'The Earth Song', 'Isn't She Lovely' and many others. 'Ebony and Ivory' was a good one. Rudra seemed to see the significance of the song. As we sang along to it, I detected his head tilting towards mine and facial expressions beginning to emerge, him spending more and more time looking at me as he sang increasingly expressively with less time looking at the road.

It was at that point that I realised that we had just gone through a very busy major road junction where everyone else had stopped on the orders of a traffic policeman who was trying to control the chaos of horns scooters motor bikes buses and cars.

Fortunately, we had been at the front of the line of traffic in the middle of three lanes, which meant there was no one to go into. As we charged through the junction past the policeman, Rudra was giving it large. Not for the first time in my life, fortune favoured me that day as we passed at thirty miles an hour between a truck and another car coming the other way, headlights flashing us in the early evening darkness. Rudra was on a different plane of consciousness. Not only had we ignored the orders of a policeman who probably had a gun and was quite annoyed, but we were also on the wrong side of the road. All of this completely unnoticed by Rudra, who, not looking at the road ahead, was still singing. I think he heard me gasp and say quite loudly, "shit!" Returning his attention to the road, he corrected his error and swerved violently to avoid a scooter, laden with driver, passenger and straw bales. "The traffic is very bad at this time," he said as we continued the last few miles through Fort to the accompaniment of Stevie Wonder singing 'You Are Not Alone'. I was quite shaken by the experience and it took a while to relax and compose myself.

Before long we found ourselves at a standstill in heavy traffic brought about by a wedding celebration. The street was almost impassable. Cars were arriving with guests, people were having photographs taken and there was singing and dancing.

It was a truly magnificent sight; everyone dressed in their best some in suits and others in traditional Indian dress. Ladies looked beautiful in their *saris* and extravagant golden jewellery. The entrance to the venue was lit up like something out of an Oscar's night in Hollywood and music filled the air. Although evening, darkness was turned to day.

Rudra stopped Stevie and opened the window so that we could hear the music and the celebrations. The air smelled of incense and perfume. Whoever these people were, they must have been very well-off, or perhaps in debt for the rest of their lives, I thought.

As we sat waiting for the traffic to move, I noticed three figures emerging ghost like from a pink mist caused by celebratory smoke flairs and fireworks. They were walking amongst the waiting traffic, begging, hands outreached with palms up as they approached the stationary cars. For the rest of my days, I will remember the child looking at me through my open window. She must have been 10. She had a grubby looking unwashed face with untidy reddish hair. I remember her eyes. They looked straight through me as if expecting nothing but holding out at least for something.

It saddens me to note how when confronted with the painful and uncomfortable realities of life we may choose to turn away. Our sense of normality disturbed we feel threatened.

It's not a physical threat. How could it be from an under-fed 10-year-old girl? It is an attack on our emotions. We are no longer in control, someone else is dictating the terms and they are spoiling the party.

I shook my head and without even giving her the dignity of eye contact, rejected her plea for money with a dismissive wave of the hand. This was one of the most shameful moments of my life.

In the midst of all those riches in that street and I include myself in that, I couldn't find it in my heart to dip into my pocket for a few rupees. What is more it was Valentine's Day. Who would tell her she was loved this evening?

My selfish reaction to a child in need was unusual for me. Somehow I had bought into the narrative of 'you just have to ignore them' so often heard from others who had previously been to India and been approached by beggars. My mind was telling me *Hey look, they do this all the time. Are you really going to fall for this?* Modern psychology calls this friction between values and actions, which do not support them as cognitive dissonance. It is painful.

Mercifully, we began to move and she was left behind. Immediately a lump came to my throat and I put my hand to my mouth to stifle a sob. Rudra understood what had just happened I am sure. Touching my arm he smiled and said, "Its OK." But it wasn't, why didn't I have the compassion to act kindly?

Before retirement from the NHS, as part of my job I helped teach mindfulness meditation exercises to patients. During that time, compassion was something of a buzzword. It has been shown to be mentally and physically beneficial for us to develop compassion in ourselves. This dreadful experience was a reminder to me that navel gazing and using words like compassion means little without action.

We arrived at the residency with a sense of relief on my part. The mood had changed and I was quiet. I thanked Rudra with a generous tip and we parted company. As he pulled away, I noticed what it was that had been rubbing. A small plastic bag had wrapped itself around something under the rear wing of his taxi. As he drove forward, the bag partially inflated with air and was making contact with the rotating wheel. It made me smile to think it would probably still be there if it was him who came to take me back to the airport for my return flight. I was beginning to cheer up.

The reception staff had been expecting me and after a few administrative formalities I was once again placed in the very capable hands of the motor biking concierge who for the first time told me his name was Raj "I have a very nice room for you," he said smiling, leading me out into the street and to a building next door. The entrance to the building was amazingly plush and the atrium decorated and designed to what looked like a very high standard. Raj punched in the door security code and we went in. He led me upstairs to the first level and proudly showed me my room. It was immaculate and appeared to be new judging by the fresh smell of newly decorated walls and paintwork. The bathroom was ultra-modern. The bedroom could only be described as luxurious.

I thanked Raj, tipping him as he left. I sat for a while admiring my plush room. That young girl's face came to me again. I wondered where she might sleep tonight and what she may eat.

After a shower and change of shirt, I felt a little happier. I made my way downstairs and walked across to the main residency reception to enquire about dinner there. Raj was standing in the reception area resplendent in his gold and white coloured high neck tunic. "Will you be eating tonight, my friend?"

I said I would.

"Come," he said, "I will take you. It will be very busy but you will have a table." How he knew there would be a table for me I don't know, however, I accepted and went with it.

The motorbike trip was once again fun, although this time without the aid of alcohol. We arrived at the same restaurant as last time. It was festooned with red heart-shaped balloons. A very long queue snaked back down the street with young couples hoping to get a table for their special Valentines night out. As we arrived, the manager who remembered me came out of the main door and greeted me, shaking my hand and smiling broadly as he ushered me into the restaurant past the queue of hopeful diners.

I said that I should queue with the rest of the customers but he insisted that my table had already been reserved for me as long as I didn't mind sharing with two others. He led me in, and seated me at a table with two other men. There wasn't much said between us after initial greetings had been exchanged.

I couldn't help but notice the looks of bemusement on the faces of couples as they filed into the restaurant whenever a table became available. Having seen me walk past them outside with the manager and now settled at a table they must have been wondering who the hell I was. I was wondering who the hell some thought I was, given the amount of attention I had received since arriving in India.

Having finished their meal, the two at my table left after half an hour of my arrival. I enjoyed a long-awaited lager, then another before ordering my meal. Allowing myself to normalise again after the journey from the airport I gave some thought about what I would do the next day, which was my final full day before my departure from India. I had wanted to visit the Mahatma Gandhi Museum in Mumbai at some point during my stay so decided that was what I would do first thing in the morning.

My meal arrived. I had ordered a Goan style fish curry, which was aromatic and medium in heat. This was accompanied by *nan* bread and cucumber rattan. It all went together well and was delicious. Time passed quickly and being tired and emotionally drained, I decided to call it a day and walk back to the residency. The manager escorted me out urging me to return again soon. The queue outside had now gone and I wondered if everyone had managed to get a table.

It was only about 20 minutes' walk to the residency from the restaurant but the walk did my knee good and helped clear my tired head a little. I was glad to be back and enjoy the comfort of the lovely room. It was very quiet and dark. Getting into the luxuriously comfortable bed I quickly dropped off to sleep.

12. Gandhi and the One-Eyed Entrepreneur

I woke at around 7:30 having had a good 8 hours sleep. Refreshed, I decided to make an early start and get to the Gandhi Visitor Centre early and be first in the queue if there happened to be one. Visiting the centre was on my list of things to do.

After a shower and putting on a fresh shirt, I skipped breakfast and made my way out into the warm morning sunshine. Having spent the night in an air-conditioned room it took time to adjust to the heat, sounds and smells of busy Mumbai.

You are never far from a taxi in Mumbai and very shortly I was negotiating a price to the centre. I arrived three quarters of an hour before opening time and there was no one else waiting. As I leaned against a low wall, a chai seller approached. I was glad to buy a 20-rupee paper cup of his delicious sweet tea, which would suffice as breakfast. As I sipped my sweet tea, I studied the impressive colonial style villa from which Gandhi directed his movement of non-cooperation against British rule. I pictured him standing on the balcony, which overlooked the street, addressing the crowds below.

The morning sun began to find its heat and before long it was time to cross the street to the shade and stand at the entrance to await its opening. By now, others had arrived and I found myself at the head of a queue of about a dozen tourists.

Finally, the gates opened and we filed in to pay our 20-rupee entrance fee. The entrance hall was met by a stairway, which led to two levels. The ground level contained the library, reception and visitor toilets. The second level had displays and a pictorial history of the great man's life journey. His living quarters consisted of a room with a simple mattress laid on the floor. There was a pillow and blankets if needed. His floor level desk sat at the foot of his bed and there was a spinning wheel in the corner of the room.

The spinning wheel was an important symbol of India's struggle for independence from British rule. Home spun cotton decreased India's reliance on Britain for the manufacture of calico. Gandhi asked everyone to spin for a short while every day. India supplied millions of tons of cotton to Britain for the manufacture of calico in Lancashire before buying it back to make clothes. Gandhi maintained that nothing in the political world was more important than spinning.

It took me around 2 hours to complete my visit. I read every notice and studied every photograph diligently. This was an important goal of my visit to India and I felt happy that it had been achieved.

It was now approaching mid-day and I decided that I would like to go back to visit the India Gate again, have some lunch and collect my shirts and trousers from the tailor. Another taxi ride through the streets of Mumbai possibly at one of its busiest times was once more exhilarating.

I took my time looking at the Gate and photographing it from every angle. This iconic symbol of British power and the influence, which the British had over such a huge country, was hard to contemplate.

The need to eat and drink was once again calling me. As I turned away from the gate to make my way to find somewhere, I heard, "Uncle, excuse me Uncle." Looking around there was a young man and his wife with a small child. They asked if they could have a photo of me with them. They had already accosted a young man and asked him to be the photographer. Happily I posed with them for the picture. The family were very grateful and left smiling looking at the photograph of themselves with a stranger.

It was now very hot and I was desperate for a beer and something to eat. The route between the India Gate and the marketplace tailor was about 35 minutes but quite straight forward.

Walking along the busy street I noticed a small crowd ahead of me blocking the pavement. There were raised voices and I could see that in the middle of the crowd there was a cow, accompanied by a young man probably in his teens and another older man in his mid-sixties perhaps. The older man was leading the cow slowly along the pavement while the younger one was begging for money.

As I approached, the crowd slowly dispersed, some looking bemused. The cow and its owners were now upon me and the young man's hand was out asking for money. What I saw horrified me. The cow was mature, a sandy colour with a kindly face. On the top of its neck, there was another cow, a small partially formed calf flopping around attached to its siblings neck like a tumour. Its head was fully formed and its open lifeless eyes looked mournfully out unseeing onto the world. Its lifeless body looked almost fully formed and was covered in the same sandy down, as its siblings. As they approached, the calf flopped from side to side with the motion. It was a horrific sight.

The poor cow was being used as a freak show. This was one of those contradictions sometimes seen in India. A sacred animal being cynically used for monetary gain.

I quickened my step and sidestepped the spectacle. Both of the men shouting after me for money hands open in plea as if the money was going to assist the cow. Cows do OK without owners in India. This poor thing was a hostage. The incident was upsetting and the image lingered for the rest of the day.

I really wanted a beer now and decided to cross the street to what looked like a more prosperous part lined with restaurants. The road was wide and the traffic as usual manic. I stood at a well-worn zebra crossing. It looked like it may have been put there in the 1950s and hadn't been painted since.

No one would ever stop to let you cross on these long-forgotten attempts at road etiquette and safety. As I stood there waiting for the right moment to attempt to cross, a woman in a *sari* who looked to be in her sixties joined me. She was standing beside me and under my breath I said, "Right Auntie, I'm following you." At that, she turned to me and said, "Yes Uncle, follow me. We are both old now and should take care."

When we got to the other side of the road, the lady engaged me in casual chitchat for a while. I could see that she had one eye. The other one was shut and looked as if it was scarred. I had heard of children in some parts of India being mutilated in order to gain sympathy for the purposes of begging. This was only hearsay, however believable. Her short thin frame and dark rugged complexion was suggestive of a hard life. Her English was good.

I said that I was on my way to find somewhere for a beer and something to eat. "I have a very nice place where you can eat and drink very cheaply."

"Come," she said, "I will show you."

Once again, like a sheep to the slaughter I allowed myself to be led through narrow alleyways past back street traders and wandering cattle before arriving at a dingy looking canteen. The dining room was small and narrow, just enough room for around eight small tables in a line pushed up against a wall with a walkway beside them. Most of the tables were occupied with people having their lunch. I noticed there was a group of four ladies at the end tables chatting and drinking what looked like chai. This was a reassuring domestic scene in the midst of yet another leap into the unknown. The canteen, however, was not for me. The one-eyed lady led me through a sliding side door into a dark room illuminated only by a television and neon flytrap. There were around five men who looked Indian sat around drinking beer. They sat gazing at the television only looking at us briefly as we walked in to take a seat.

I ordered a beer, which a waiter brought. It was opened and poured in front of me this time. I recalled my last invitation to go for a cheap beer and meal. The lady wanted nothing. I paid the waiter who lingered for a while before I realised he was waiting for a tip, which I duly gave.

It was congenial enough as I sat drinking my beer and making small talk realising immediately of course that this was a sting and that I had only minutes before it would unfold.

She told me that she was from the slums and came to work each day at this canteen to earn money for her children. Her husband was dead and she was the only breadwinner. The story was heartrending and if true reflected the desperate situation many millions find themselves in Mumbai.

Finishing my beer I felt it was time to move on. I didn't want to eat there. I thanked her for showing me the place and gave her 500 rupees for her children. "OK," she said, "but first come with me I will show you something you will like."

What now? I thought.

Walking out of the dingy drinking room into the canteen then out into the street, I felt relieved to be in the open air again. Come, come, she said hurrying on in front of me like the rabbit in Louis Carol's *Alice*. I followed reluctantly now, my knee sore from all the walking I had done.

I decided at that moment to split, but just as I was about to walk off, I found myself being ushered into a very modern, clean air-conditioned tailor's shop. I sensed my conditioning to western ways, as I longed to be comfortable again.

The owner greeted me enthusiastically. "I must say," I said quickly, raising my hand in a gesture of determination, "I have no intentions of buying anything." He looked hurt.

"My friend," he said, "my intention is not to sell you anything. I am proud of my shop and my good friend here who you have already met thought you may appreciate seeing some of the fine fabrics and clothes I make." I looked at one-eyed Aunty who looked at me smiling and nodding.

"First, my friend, would you like a beer or chai?" I respectfully declined since I didn't want this to develop into a comfy situation that I would find even harder to get out of. I cursed myself for allowing this to happen in the first place.

Aunty stood in the background as the tailor proceeded to bring out bundles of fine linen of every texture and colour. I looked on with fake admiration. Bundles of cloth are not my cup of chai.

Eventually and inevitably the subject of shirts trousers and suits came about. At that, I lost patience and stood to go. I must go I said. I have much to do. The tailor was now trying with all of his might to engage me in looking at shirt designs assuring me that they would be ready for collection in one hour. I cursed one eyed aunty who had sprung this trap, and ignoring the rising tempo of the tailor and obvious obstructive body language of aunty standing in front of the door, I pushed past her and escaped out into the street.

They both came out after me calling, "Please wait! We can do a very special deal for you." My pace quickened and soon I had left them behind, angry with myself for not having learned yet.

This was yet another example of someone doing something for payment then generating business for someone else who in turn would reward you for your efforts. A sort of pyramid business, I guess.

Having escaped my self-made trap I made for the nearest restaurant for some lunch before picking up my shirts and trousers. Lunch was tempura pannier and lemon slices accompanied by a large Kingfisher. It was delightful to sit there and relax after such an eventful day. As I enjoyed the moment, I reflected on what had happened that day, smiling to myself at my achievements and frowning at my gullibility.

Following lunch I made my way to the incredibly busy marketplace which for me was a landmark enabling me to easily find my way to the tailor. The brightly coloured stalls, sounds and aromas of burning incense and street food were a heady mix.

I soon found the side-street where the tailor's shop was, remembering his promise that he would sell me a suit. My experience of the previous few hours hardened my resolve against any attempts to influence me and I entered the shop with determination.

To my delight the owner wasn't there. I gave the assistant my receipt and he fetched my clothes, all neatly presented in a paper carrier bag. Thanking him, I left the shop smartly.

It was now late afternoon and time to get back to the residency to rest and scrub up before the evening. The taxi ride to the residency was slow at this time of the day, with the usual commuter activity seen in any big city anywhere in the world I thanked the driver, tipped him and went up to my room.

When I got to my room, I found that it had been carefully made up. The clothes, which I had sent for washing, had been returned and there was a note on the bedside saying 'hello, please look in fridge'. In the fridge there were three large bottles of Kingfisher lager, which Raj had promised to get for me. I had already given him enough money to buy it and by way of a 'thank you' I didn't intend taking any change. I had forgotten about the lager and it was a delightful surprise.

I spent the last couple of hours enjoying my lager, listening to music on my phone and ironing my freshly laundered clothes.

At around 6:30, I made my way to the reception in the building next door. I needed to confirm my transport to the airport for the next day and see Raj to thank him for the lager and ensure he received a generous tip for looking after me so well. My flight the next day was at 1 pm. I was advised to get there three hours before departure and allowing for an hours journey in case of hold ups, the taxi arranged by the residency would collect me at 8 am. I asked for a 7am call.

Raj was there, and as ever smiling ear to ear, eager to perform his last beyond the call of duty concierge act and take me for one last spin on his motor bike to his friend's restaurant.

Contented that everything for my return to the airport in the morning was arranged I turned to Raj who smiled and said, "Let's go my friend." Climbing onto the back of the bike for the last time was a little sad as I knew I would have to find my own way back again and that this was likely to be the last motorbike ride I would have for a very long time if ever.

We set off with a sudden acceleration. Raj was going to make my last ride a memorable one. No one was going to hold us up, not even a holy cow. Engine revving high through numerous gear changes and horn sounding almost continuously it seemed we charged through the narrow streets like a scene from a James Bond movie. It was truly breath-taking. The adrenaline was pumping through my body so much so that when we arrived and I got off the bike, my legs shook. I'm not sure about my hands because they always shake.

I thanked Raj tipping him well and telling him to keep the change from the lager. He was very pleased indeed with the tip and told me I was a 'very good man'. Off he went, back to the residency never to be seen again.

There was the usual warm welcome when I entered the restaurant. I dined alone initially, ordering the same as the previous evening since there was nothing else on the menu which inspired me. later, the restaurant owner who obviously delighted in playing my host introduced a couple to me who had recently done a tour of the holy land and had been staying in Israel. India was their next adventure.

They were from Dublin and were travelling as part of their honeymoon. The man told me he was an archaeologist specialising in the early Middle East. She was a college lecturer and yoga teacher. They both looked middle aged.

Their intention was to travel across India, as far as possible by train. They hoped to reach the Himalayas and find a yoga retreat there.

They were an interesting couple and I was fascinated with their stories about their time in the holy land and the man's archaeological work

The evening passed quickly and looking at my phone I could see it was fast approaching my bed time. Worn out after the day's events I left my fellow travellers to it. The manager was nowhere to be seen this time so after paying my bill I was able to slip away quietly; but not before becoming entangled in the entrance door fly chain curtain again for old time sake.

On my walk back to the residency, I reflected upon all that had happened since my arrival in India. I had experienced so much and had met many people who I am sure I would never forget. I wondered if they would remember me.

I was glad to get back to my room. I was so very tired after that last day in Mumbai and climbing into my bed, sleep came quickly.

Refreshed, I woke at 6.30 beating my 7am call. With a sense of sadness coupled with looking forward to going home, I made a cup of tea, got my stuff together, showered and shaved and said farewell to my lovely room.

The reception staff were as helpful as ever. I paid my final bill, which included my taxi ride to the airport, and they handed me back my passport. Thanks and farewells were made and I stepped out of the residency for the last time to my taxi. Unfortunately it wasn't Rudra the performing cabbie. I would have been delighted if it was.

The trip to the airport was without incident. The driver spoke no English at all, so silence was not awkward and allowed me to daydream about my experiences over the past 13 days. I remember thinking that I would like to return to India again one day but next time I would do things differently.

Check-in was straightforward. Once again, I said goodbye to my rucksack. This time I was less anxious about letting it go. By the time I had passed through security and walked to the departure gates, I didn't have much longer to wait before boarding.

We were a mixed bunch waiting at the gate. Indian ladies in brightly coloured *saris* some quite elderly with their grey hair neatly combed back into a bun. Others were young with children, some of whom already looked restless. Recalling the screaming child I wondered if there would be a repeat performance of my flight from London. Announcements in

English referring to London Heathrow, was confirmation that my India adventure was at an end.

The time came and we were asked to board. My seat was the one I had paid extra for. It was by the emergency exit door and I was in the window seat. Disappointingly the window was actually behind my right shoulder so I had to strain my neck to look out of it. In retrospect, I would have been better off having an ordinary window seat. At least I had plenty of legroom though, which was helpful for my painful knee.

Beside me to my left was a middle age Indian couple. They acknowledged me with a smile as I took my seat. After a lot of shifting around and arranging things then rearranging things then getting up again to get something or another from their bag in the overhead locker, we all settled down for the 9-hour flight to Heathrow.

Looking out of the window over my right shoulder I followed our trundle along the tarmac to take our place in the queue of other aircraft waiting to take off. Finally, the engines roared to life and we were away. As we climbed through the cloud of pollution, which blanketed Mumbai into the clear blue sky above, I watched India disappear beneath me.

The flight was comfortable. We made good time and the entertainment screen in front kept me informed about the route and our progress. As with the flight out, the drinks were served prior to eating. I stuck to a miniature bottle of red wine before lunch, one with and one for after to settle down and watch a film. My neighbours could put it away. Whisky was their choice and there seemed to be a constant flow of the stuff.

Flying into darkness, there wasn't much to see. I was leaving blue skies and 34 degrees temperatures for 2°C freezing fog and in some places snow. It was going to be a shock to the system when I got back.

After crossing Europe and then the English Channel, we began to descend. Lights on the costal land below us shone through the darkness, their density increasing as each minute passed.

I reflected on my visit to India as I gazed out of the window. I remember thinking of how it had turned out to be quite different to how I imagined it would be. I never intended to have the amount of human interaction that I had. The speed with which casual interactions blossomed into friendships between complete strangers was astounding really. I suppose it says something about people needing people. A retreat or *ashram* would have done it I suppose, however, my values in life are around fun, laughter, exploration and adventure. A retreat sounded dull in comparison to those values.

Returning my gaze from the window and the ever-brightening lights of London below me I readied myself for landing. I was looking forward to being home again but I had a sense of something unfinished and was sure I would return to India again at least one more time.

As I was travelling back to the UK, I was unaware of the catastrophe which was unfolding in India and the rest of the World. Covid-19 was yet to emerge as the world's greatest health and economic challenge since World War 2.

Within 3 months of returning to the UK, India was closed to the outside world. The disease had permeated every aspect of life there.

In the last months of 2022, I am pleased to record that India again opened its doors to travellers. With grateful thanks to the scientists who created the vaccines which freed us from the tyranny of this disease, we are once again good to go!

Notes

1. Maharashtra is the second most populous state in India. It is the state's capital and Nagpur is the winter capital. Maharashtra is rich in history and archaeology. It is home to four UNESCO world heritage sites. These are the Ajanta, Ellora, and Elephanta caves and the Chhatrapti Shivaji Maharaj Terminus (CSTM). The Ajanta caves consist of 30 rock-cut Buddhist cave monuments dating back to the 2nd century BCE. The Ellora caves are one of the largest rock-cut Hindu temple cave complexes in the world. The Elephanta caves are dedicated to the Hindu god Shiva. They are on an island, which is 10 miles outside of Mumbai harbour. There are plenty of boats, which take tourists there.
2. Kerala's history is interesting. It has been prominent in the spice trade for over 5000 years and has seen ancient traders visit its shores from as far away as Greece and Sumeria, which is now southern Iraq. Later, in the 16th century, Portuguese traders landed on its shores to trade. It soon became clear to them that Kerala was not only rich in spices but was also important strategically.

Eventually Kerala was occupied and subdued by the Portuguese who brought with them their Christian churches and culture, much of which can be seen along stretches of the west coast including Goa. Agonda is a large fishing village. In 1510, the Portuguese exerted their religious influences on the population and imposed Catholicism. Hinduism and Christianity now sit comfortably together in this peaceful place.

3. In 1837, the first trains were used in India for transporting granite for road building. The first passenger train ran in 1853 and carried around 400 passengers a distance of 21 miles between Bombay and Thane, the oldest section of rail in India and active today unlike many of the lines and stations in Britain which were axed in the 1960s. Following the introduction of those first granite trains and for the next 180 years, trains became woven into the very fabric of life in India. In so doing, they produced a social class intimately entwined with iron and steam.

These days, the Indian railway network is the fourth largest in the world, employing 1.25 million workers and supporting many small businesses. Among the more visible businesses are the Mumbai Dabbawalas and more widely seen, the *chai* sellers. Dabbawalas or tiffin carriers, operate a highly efficient system delivering lunches. The lunches are packed in dabbas, which are round tin containers approximately 10 inches in diameter. Each tin has a lid and on it there is a unique stencil or mark which tells the Dabawala where it is to be delivered and to whom. The lunches are prepared at home, or by caterers for delivery to workers every day of the year, all over Mumbai. The dabbas are collected, delivered and then returned empty to their origin. It is an incredibly efficient system and very few go missing or are incorrectly delivered in a year. The operation is unique to Mumbai and is run as a cooperative.

Ingram Content Group UK Ltd.
Milton Keynes UK
UKHW020638220623
423865UK00011B/587